After-Death Communications:

GOD'S GIFT OF LOVE

CHRISTINE DUMINIAK

After-Death Communications: God's Gift of Love
Christine Duminiak
www.ChristineDuminiak.com

Cover Art by Jackie Kern
Cover Design by AlyBlue Media, LLC
Interior Design by AlyBlue Media LLC
Published by AlyBlue Media, LLC
Copyright © 2017 by Christine Duminiak. All rights reserved. No part of this publication may be reproduced, distributed or transmitted in any form or by any means, without prior written permission of the publisher.

ISBN: 978-1-944328-70-2
AlyBlue Media, LLC
Ferndale, WA 98248
www.AlyBlueMedia.com

All rights reserved. No part of this book may be reproduced or transmitted in any form or by any means, electronic or mechanical, including photocopying, recording, or by any information storage and retrieval system, without permission in writing from the copyright owner. Scripture citation is from the Holy Bible, New International Version, Copyright © 1973, 1978, 1984 by International Bible Society. All rights reserved worldwide.

Front cover painting by artist Jax (Jackie Kern). E-mail Jax at jaxsayk@gmail.com. Jax says, "My paintings are one big ADC, with each one taking me on a wonderful journey and giving me a peek into Heaven . . . What an incredibly peaceful place to be."

PRINTED IN THE UNITED STATES OF AMERICA

AFTER-DEATH COMMUNICATIONS

Experts Praise

"**EXTRAORDINARILY COMFORTING** . . . For those who wonder if afterlife visits are possible, these stories reassure us that even after death our loved ones remain an important part of our lives. This is the perfect book for the newly bereaved and others who want to learn more about this mysterious topic." -DR. GLORIA HORSLEY, President, Open to Hope Foundation. -DR. HEIDI HORSLEY, Adjunct Professor, School of Social Work, Columbia University, Author, Co-Founder of Open to Hope Organization. The Compassionate Friends National Board of Directors, and Advisory Board for the Tragedy Assistance Program for Survivors of Military Loss (TAPS)

"**OUTSTANDING** . . . This is an outstanding book for all, whether grieving or not. If you are grieving, you will find specific information that can be of immense use in coping with your great loss." -LOUIS E. LAGRAND, Ph.D., CT, author of *Loves Lives On*.

"**A TREASURE** . . . This book is a treasure for all those who yearn to remember we don't die!" -JUDITH GUGGENHEIM, co-founder and researcher of the ADC Project and co-author of *Hello From Heaven*.

"**OUTSTANDING AND COMPELLING** . . . Will bring healing, comfort, and hope to those who grieve. I can't recommend it too highly! Absolutely wonderful!" -SUNNI WELLES, Christian Spiritual Medium, radio host of Ask The Angels Show and author of *Glimpses of Heaven From the Angels Who Live There*.

"**FASCINATING** . . . Life-altering afterlife stories and insights. This excellent self-help book is a must for anyone who is grieving! -JOSEPH F. WRIGHT, C.H.T., I.A.C.T., International Clinical Hypnotherapist, creator of the Awaken Your Inner Healer Seminars, author of *Transcripts From The Psychic Hypnotist*.

AFTER-DEATH COMMUNICATIONS

Dedication

To Our Loving Father, Jesus and the Holy Spirit, Who inspired this book, and who have always made me feel so extremely loved and cared for, even in my darkest hours. May all Your "kids" come to know just how very special, greatly loved, and treasured they are by You. Thank You for everything.

Contents

PART I – INTRODUCTION

1	My Guardian Angel's Prophecy	3
2	Spirit Communication in the Bible	17
3	20 Types of Afterlife Signs & Tips	27

PART II – AFTER-DEATH COMMUNICATION STORIES

4	Visits From Jesus Christ	41
5	Angels	49
6	Audio: Voices, Music & Sounds	57
7	Birds, Animals & Insects	73
8	Children's Experiences	85
9	Coins	95
10	Comas	101
11	Computers	109
12	Dreams From Adults	115
13	Dreams From Children	121
14	Electrical	133
15	Forgiveness	145
16	Godincidences	155

17	Healings	163
18	Help	173
19	Lost & Found	181
20	Unexplained Objects	189
21	Out of Body Experiences	197
22	Phones, Texts, Caller IDs, & Answering Machines	203
23	Scents	213
24	Suicides & Afterlife Visits	221
25	Visions of Adults	231
26	Visions of Children	239
27	Pet Visitations	243
28	Warnings & Premonitions	257

PART III – HEALING FROM GRIEF

| 29 | Why Do Bad Things Happen to Good People? | 269 |

- Your Soul Agreement
- Straying From Your Soul Agreement
- Choosing One's Death
- Survivors Guilt
- Suicides and the Power of Prayers
- Anger at God

| 30 | Grief Healing Advice | 283 |

- Is My Loved One Okay?
- Who Met My Loved One?
- Talk To Them
- They Still See And Hear You
- Our Children
- Where Do Pets Go?

- Goodbye, I Love You & Forgiveness
- Happily Remembering Them
- The Hug Pillow & Quilt
- Journal Your ADCs
- Laughter
- Feeling Guilty About Reinvesting In Life
- Service To Others
- Wanting More Afterlife Signs
- Spiritual Mediums
- Grieving
- Earth Is A Temporary Residence

Resources	295
Acknowledgements	299
About Christine Duminiak	303

Author's Note

Dear Reader,

Even though a number of these stories are from enthusiastic Christians, there are also some from the Jewish and Muslim faiths, as well as those who don't identify with any specific religion. This book is not meant to proselytize Christianity to you. Rather, it was meant to bring awareness of the common types of afterlife contacts and signs, and the role of prayer in receiving afterlife signs, so that you can learn how to recognize and receive your own.

All these stories are true events, even though in some cases the names may be masked to protect the privacy of the contributors.

PART I

Introduction

CHAPTER 1

My Guardian Angel's Prophecy

The Apparition

"Bob, Bob, your parents are here! Your parents are here! Wake up! Wake up!" This was my very emotional and exuberant cry to my sound asleep hubby, as I was shaking his arm trying to get his attention, when I realized his DEAD parents were standing in our bedroom!

It was March 19, 1998, and my dear deceased father-in-law and mother-in-law, John and Stella, were visiting us in our bedroom at 4 a.m. However, the remarkable thing was that John had *died* in 1987, and his wife Stella had *passed on* in 1993. I would like to back-up a little bit here and explain to the reader what happened a few minutes prior to my in-laws' spirits visiting, so you can get the full picture of the wondrous evening I was having, which was my first spiritual contact ever with the "dead."

I had just awoken from a dream and glanced at the clock to see what time it was. I noticed it was 4 a.m. Much to my satisfaction, I realized that I still had two more hours left to get some shut-eye before my alarm would go off at 6 a.m. As I settled my weary head back down on my comfy pillow expecting to return to dreamland, something in the room caught my eye that made my heart instantly start to pound. I stared in disbelief. I saw a "man" in the room! He wasn't just standing in the room though; he was sitting at a desk, which was SUSPENDED IN SPACE NEAR THE CEILING!

This "man" was very solid looking and dressed in a red cloak with a black, large-brimmed hat, similar to the style that an Italian padre would wear on his head. While sitting at this desk, suspended in space, he seemed extremely peaceful, as he was holding an open book in his hands in a serene and prayerful manner.

The whole scene looked similar to a 3-D movie or a hologram. My heart continued to race as I wondered what the heck was happening in my bedroom and who was this man! I was hoping the unexplainable would just disappear if I blinked my eyes a few times—but he didn't disappear right away—for God had other plans for me.

After about fifteen very long seconds, which was time enough for me to realize that this apparition was indeed for real, this very peaceful "Italian padre" sitting near my ceiling suddenly dissipated into a red, misty haze, which lingered in the air. Even though the apparition of the "padre" had been very peaceful and quiet, after the padre vanished, there were now some new spirits in the room. These new spirits did not look like the "good guys" or the "padre" though, and they caused me to feel alarmed.

So I reached for my rosary beads from under my pillow. I started to pray for God's help and protection. Nothing supernatural had ever happened to me before, and my brain was trying to logically compute these paranormal events and to make some sense out of it.

As I continued to pray, I heard a gush of wind blow into the room and papers being rustled on my bureau, even though all the windows in the house were closed. At the same time, my bedroom momentarily turned a soft, bluish color, dashed with flashes of white, twinkling lights. Next I caught a glimpse of the head of a woman, hovered over my bedroom doorway. She wore a white veil covering her hair, similar to the way the Blessed Mother dressed back in the days when Jesus Christ walked the earth. She looked at me, as if to reassure me that everything was safe now, and then she vanished. The brief sight of her presence and the instant removal of the not-so-nice-looking spirits, filled me with an immediate sense of calm and serenity; I now realized I had nothing to fear, that God had answered my prayers for His protection.

While contemplating the wonderment of it all, I noticed there were now some other vague-looking spirits in the room at the foot of my bed. They were not scary though. They had no definitive form, and their appearance reminded me of red-colored radio waves floating in the air. By now I was not only relaxed, but curious too. I started to calmly reflect on what spirit would want to visit me! The only member of my immediate family that I lost was one I had never even met (a four-month pregnancy 13 years prior), who I was no longer grieving, and whose passing I had long ago accepted. I had not lost any close friends nor any immediate family members since then. So I wasn't grieving anyone at the time of this spiritual visit. Then it came to me! I remembered that my husband had grieved very long and hard for his dad (John) after John had returned back Home to God, eleven years earlier.

I felt a strong impulse to call out to John, so I said, "John, is that you?" It was as if John was just hanging back waiting for some recognition and permission to approach me. As soon as I asked that question, one of the spirits immediately got stronger and took on a more definitive shape. Suddenly John was floating a few inches in front of my face. I could now see him from his chest up. He appeared semitransparent in density, and he was sporting a black fedora style hat, white dress shirt, black suit coat, a striped tie, and a white hankie in his coat pocket. I could see John, yet I could see through him! I became really excited when I realized that I had guessed correctly and dear sweet John was actually there in our bedroom!

Then I thought, well John and Stella (his wife) always traveled together, so . . . . I then asked John if Stella was there with him? As soon as I asked John that question, I saw another hat! This time it was a woman's hat, reminiscent of the flappers of the Roaring Twenties. The flapper's hat was floating in front of John's fedora. Stella was wearing the flapper's hat. She had on red lipstick and wore white pearls around her neck. Her face had a chalky white appearance, even though she, too, was semitransparent. One minute John and Stella would be at the foot of my bed, and the next instant they would be five inches in front of my face. It was amazing how quickly they could travel.

I was so happy and excited to see them. It was then that I finally remembered about my husband, who was sleeping very soundly by my side throughout this whole captivating, supernatural experience.

So I woke him up exclaiming, "Bob, Bob, your parents are here! Your parents are here! Wake up! Wake up!" My cries of excitement woke Bob up and he looked for his parents, but he didn't seem to have the ability to be able to see them, as I did. I could tell that my husband believed me though. As he struggled to focus in on where I was pointing, Bob was smiling in acknowledgment of his parents' presence anyway. He was moving his lips silently praying to them. As I gazed in amazement at my in-laws' spirits, I, too, found myself talking to them silently and telling them how thrilled and honored I was that they had come to visit us. Because I was not able to hear their voices, nor their thoughts, I continued to keep up a one-sided conversation, all the while smiling and giggling in delight. After a while my husband fell back to sleep and I continued staring and talking to them. Finally, it was now close to 5 a.m., and they had been there for close to an hour. I could no longer keep my eyes open, so I apologized to them and said I was going to go back to sleep. I thanked them for coming and waved goodbye to them. They waved back at me! I was elated!

The next morning I told my husband the whole story from beginning to end. I also traveled to my parents' home to share this mystical experience with them. My parents, who were in their late 70s, loved hearing all about it and were just as excited as I was. What I most loved about my parents' reaction was that they believed me unquestionably, even though they had never heard of, nor experienced anything supernatural like this either. How comforting it was to be able to share something so important with them and to have them be so accepting and supportive of it and me.

The Quest For Answers

I didn't know at the time, though, that there was much more to come in the way of John and Stella's visits. The very next night when I went to bed, guess who arrived again? Yep, John and Stella. They continued to come back a few times a week, yet I didn't know why. Because I couldn't hear their voices or thoughts, I started to get a little worried that they may be trying to get a warning to me about my husband's health. You see, my husband had a scary bout with cancer a few years prior to this, and the doctors thought they had caught the cancer in the beginning stages and that all was well. But now that my in-laws' spirits were visiting frequently, I wondered about my husband's health and needed to find out why my in-laws kept returning. I encouraged my husband to get a checkup, just in case, and I started on a quest to get an answer to my question—Why were my in-laws continually visiting me?

Not sure where to find the answers, I turned to the Internet, and I prayed for God's guidance and help in all of this. My search eventually led me to Judith Guggenheim. Judith with her husband Bill had done extensive research on after-death communications. They coauthored the enlightening and groundbreaking book *Hello From Heaven*, in which they explained that an after-death communication (ADC) is a spiritual experience which occurs when you are contacted directly and spontaneously by a deceased family member or friend, without the use of psychics, mediums, rituals, or devices.

Realizing that Judith Guggenheim would certainly understand my spiritual experience, I e-mailed her and asked for her help and guidance. Judith was a lifesaver to me, even though I was a perfect stranger to her. She recommended that I get in touch with a woman who was extremely gifted at being able to communicate directly with angels and other good spirits. That highly gifted woman's name is Sunni Welles, who is a Christian spiritual medium, and who does sessions with those of all faiths www.sunniwelles.com.

The Spiritual Medium

I contacted Sunni Welles and told her that I wished to contact my guardian angel. I felt that my angel would know more about me than anyone else regarding my life and why all this was happening. Being a practicing Catholic though, we are discouraged from using mediums. Since I had never ventured into anything spiritual like this before, I was a bit apprehensive about communicating with my guardian angel through a medium. However, after contacting Sunni Welles, I felt tremendously relieved. I found out that Sunni Welles was a Christian with similar beliefs to mine, even though she does readings for those of all faiths. Sunni explained that she very carefully tests the angels and spirits before her sessions, according to the way it advises in the Bible (1 John 4:1-3). She said this was the way her own angels taught her how to do this, to ensure that she was talking to spirits from the Light who were from God's spiritual realms.

I was further comforted when Sunni explained how to protect myself from unwanted spirits who were also visiting me. She taught me to rebuke Satan in the name of Jesus Christ and to ask the Lord for His protection. As a Catholic, I felt Sunni Welles' gifts were truly from the Holy Spirit as written about in the Bible (1 Corinthians 12: 3-11). I knew then that God had led me to Sunni Welles. This session with my guardian angel, through this unique and highly gifted Christian medium, proved to be profoundly life-altering for me.

During this amazing session with Sunni Welles and my guardian angel, all of my questions were answered and my angel was extremely loving, patient, helpful and kind.

My guardian angel explained to me that my in-laws were only coming by to say, "Hello," and that I had nothing to fear concerning their visits. He also explained that the "Italian padre" spirit I saw was actually a messenger angel, paving the way for my in-laws' visit that night. My guardian angel also made a prediction about my life's work here on earth. He explained that I would be helping people spiritually, emotionally and eventually with the gift of touch healing. He asked me if I would accept this mission from God. I was amazed at this revelation. Even though I felt so unworthy of such a mission, I thought, "How can I possibly refuse if God wants me to do this?" So, of course, I agreed.

I also wondered how could all of this possibly come about? I was just an ordinary mom, whose prior working experience had only been in the business world working for the President of an environmental company. Before I had a chance to question my angel further about my concerns, my angel made some helpful suggestions to get me pointed in the right direction, so that I could begin using this gift of touch healing.

I followed my angel's suggestions and eventually became a Certified Reflexologist and Energy Healer. I noticed that the clients who were coming to me seemed to be almost exclusively the bereaved. I realized that I was meant to work with the bereaved. So later I became a Certified Grief Recovery Specialist, a radio co-host with Sunni Welles (the Christian medium I had first contacted in 1998), a speaker at national seminars, and an author on a number of books about afterlife contacts. My profession also afforded me the opportunity to volunteer to help cancer and hospice patients with their pain and with spiritual counseling.

Continued Spirit Contacts

Although I do not consider myself to be a psychic or a medium, my *dead* in-laws continued to visit me from time to time. I found out that at that time in 1998 they were part of my angel team. My precious dad passed in 2000, and he also visits me. My dear mother passed in 2004 and she too visits me often through the use of afterlife signs.

Both of my parents use music, birds, touches, coins, dreams, and many of the 20 common types of afterlife signs that I have described in Chapter 3 of this book. My parents are now on my angel team and have since replaced my in-laws.

At times, even my guardian angel will make his presence known by giving me a message to help with guidance in my life. These angelic visits will usually come as a result of a prayer and the visit will be in my mind's eye or in my dream state.

These spiritual visits have been a tremendous source of joy and comfort in my life, especially since my beloved dad and mom have crossed over, and I thank God with all my heart for allowing them.

The Founding of Prayer Wave for After-Death Communication

I would like to share more about my guardian angel's prophecy about my helping people spiritually and emotionally has come about, and why I am writing this book about after-death communications (ADCs).

Since my first spiritual visit back in 1998, I have come across many others who also have received direct ADCs from their loved ones. However, sadly, I also have come across many people who were grieving intensely who never had an ADC, but desperately longed to have one. I could see a noticeable difference in the outlook and emotional state of those who received ADCs, and those who didn't.

Those who were receiving spiritual contact and signs seemed to project an inner peace and joy. They said that they felt that the signs were a validation that their loved ones were okay and safely in Heaven. They seemed to also understand that their loved ones were still around them in a spiritual way, and that they continued to share a deep and loving connection in their lives. Even though the relationship was a different one now, many times it was a more meaningful one.

These ADCs brought them elation and comfort whenever they received one. They had hope in their hearts that they would be receiving another contact or sign at some point in the future, and this gave them something to look forward to and to smile about. They seemed to understand that their loved ones saw and heard them and were still a huge part of their lives. They understood that their loved ones did not go off into a "black hole" never to be heard from again, but rather, they were still connected and their loved ones even seemed like their own guardian angel at times! Many seemed to recognize that their loved ones, who were back Home with God, had supernatural powers now, and they could be with God and with them too! They were being shown by their loved ones, time and again, that they were very interested in their lives and they got to see and hear it all here on earth! They are routing for us! They encourage us! They pray for us! They love to see us happy. They never miss a wedding, birthday, anniversary, birth, graduation, or any special occasion that is important to us, for it is important to them also.

I personally felt so immensely blessed at the on-going spiritual contacts and signs I was still receiving two years after my in-laws' first visit, and then later from my dad, that I started to feel a deep desire to do something to help others who were suffering and longed to receive after-death contacts too. Although I realize that God grants these spiritual visits and signs as gifts from His heart without our having to ask for them, I also strongly believe in "For where two or three come together in my name, there am I with them." (Matt. 18:20). With this in mind and believing in the awesome power of group prayer, I felt that if many of us banded together and started praying unselfishly for each other, and that if we stormed

Heaven in a group Prayer Wave to ask for after-death communications (ADCs) to be given to those who longed for them, that God's most loving and generous heart would be touched and moved in our favor.

So in September 2000, I felt guided to ask others to join with me in a Prayer Wave and our new nondenominational group was formed. We call ourselves "Prayer Wave For After-Death Communication."

A very dear and special friend Jenny Flores (nicknamed JO), took it upon herself to surprise me and our new nondenominational group Prayer Wave For After-Death Communication by creating for us our very own website and message board. Thanks to Jenny we had a home in which to meet on the internet, no matter what part of the world we were from!

Every Friday we storm Heaven by praying for each other in our group to get a comforting after-death communication. We simply say our own little prayer to our one Creator in our own personal way. God has been blessing our group and we have been receiving many wonderful ADCs, thanks to His kindness.

Our prayer and grief support group has since moved from a message board to a Facebook Group now called After Death Communications and Prayer Wave. Being a grief support website, and we lift each other up with words of love, compassion, encouragement, and prayers, as well as to share our wondrous ADC experiences when we receive them. We try and help others who have questions about their spiritual contacts too. Many people have shared that they had dark thoughts of suicide, because of their deep grief. But after we prayed for them and they received an afterlife sign, they lost those destructive thoughts. Our nondenominational group is open to all faiths and to all who want to join in the awesome power of group prayer for ADCs. Please consider joining our compassionate, loving and supportive private Facebook group. Facebook.com/groups/Afterdeathcommunicationsprayerwave

Through the blessings of ADCs, God has kindly revealed to us that we continue to have on-going, never-ending, loving relationships, no matter where our loved ones reside. Some refer to this spiritual connection of love between Heaven and earth as the Communion of Saints. Some refer to ADCs as a religious, sacred, mystical, supernatural or paranormal experience. Whatever label you want to give it, the ties of love can never be broken. Love is all-important to God for "God is love." (1 John 4:15) One day we "temps" here on earth will be reunited hugging and kissing spirit-to-spirit when we all return back to Heaven with God, our permanent place of residence for all eternity.

Why This Book Was Written

Some of the roadmaps of guidance along our life's journey can come from hearing the same suggestions repeatedly from others. This happened to me. Many of our Prayer Wave for After-Death Communication members kept encouraging me to write a book about their ADC experiences. I finally started to take notice of their repeated recommendations and wondered if I should give it more serious consideration.

Then I began to receive spiritual visions that a book was to be written about afterlife contacts. I prayed fervently about these visions and asked God for more affirmations if He truly wanted me to take on such an enormous project as a book. In answer to my prayers, in the forthcoming days I received more visions to go forward with this book and even to include the words "God" and "Gift" on the front cover, hence, the name of the book, *After-Death Communications: God's Gift of Love.*

I believe that all things are possible with our loving God. I believe that God wanted you to know, through this book, that there *is* eternal life. That He allows these beautiful and wondrous spiritual visits and signs, as loving gifts for our comfort and healing. I believe our Heavenly Father cares very deeply about our sorrow, and through His gifts of after-death communications, He is wrapping His loving arms around His children, "His kids," to comfort us through our grief, until we are all reunited with Him and our loved ones once more.

Our Prayer Wave For After-Death Communication members and friends enthusiastically agreed to share their beautiful after-death communication experiences with all of you, to give your heart hope, so that you will know that God does hear your prayers, and that these comforting visits truly are spiritual gifts from Him.

We hope you enjoy reading our spiritual experiences, as much as we enjoyed sharing them. It is our hope that you will begin to recognize and trust the signs you may be receiving from your loved ones, through God's grace, and that one day you too can shout your joyful experiences to the world in order to share the good news!

May God bless you all.

In Christ's Love,

CHRISTINE MARIE DUMINIAK
Certified Grief Recovery Specialist
CHRISDUMINIAK@AOL.COM | WWW.CHRISTINEDUMINIAK.COM

AFTER-DEATH COMMUNICATIONS

* * *

CHAPTER 2

Spirit Communication in the Bible

As a Catholic, I understand that Christian believers often worry that they may be sinning against God or opening the door to the occult if they are getting afterlife contacts. That almost anything having to do with afterlife contacts can be considered taboo by clergy and other believers.

Since 1998 when my *dead* in-laws visited me in my bedroom one night and stayed for an hour, I have contacted some clergy who are very familiar and supportive of afterlife contacts. I have also been contacted by people of many different faiths who have been gifted to be able to see, hear, and even communicate very naturally with spirits. I have found that children have a natural God-given gift to see and hear spirits. This was the reason why I wrote the book, *Heaven Talks To Children: Afterlife Contacts, Spiritual Gifts and Loving Messages*, to give guidance to parents of these children.

This chapter offers reassurance to Christians who have received a comforting afterlife contact or sign. It is also for those who are feeling anxious and confused if they have a gift to see, hear, and communicate with spirits. I have a much more detailed chapter on the Bible and spirit communication in my book *Heaven Talks To Children*, I wanted to touch upon this subject in this book too. Catholics do acknowledge and honor the many recognized formal saints and angels who have made apparitions from Heaven to give messages and to bring healing and help from God. However, many Catholics and clergy are not aware of the Vatican's favorable stance on afterlife contacts from "informal" saints, who are our departed loved ones residing in Heaven.

Although it is not widely known by Catholic clergy and laymen, John Hooper of the *London Observer Service* in January 1999 reported that the Reverend Gino Concetti, who was the chief theological commentator for the Vatican newspaper *L'Osservatore Romano*, said that the Roman Catholic Church believes in the feasibility of the dead being able to communicate with the living because of the Communion of Saints. Reverend Concetti stated that the Church believes that communication is possible between those who live on this earth and those who live in a state of eternal repose, in Heaven or Purgatory. Reverend Concetti further advised that it may even be that God lets our loved ones send us messages to guide us at certain moments in our lives.

Some Christians, who have shared their mystical encounters with me, have also expressed sadness and isolation because they had experienced condemnation by their church leaders and members. Some of their well-meaning churches did not recognize their spiritual experiences or gifts as being from the Holy Spirit. Some were told that *all* these contacts were from Satan and were warned to cease and desist.

As a consequence of the criticism received, some of these God-loving and very gifted Christians have felt turned off towards their churches. Some have even left their Christian faith for other more accepting belief systems. Yet these Christians wholeheartedly believed that their gifts or experiences were from God's Holy Spirit, and that these gifts should be pursued even if their church leaders did not agree with them.

It is distressing to me that even in the twenty-first century people are still being judged negatively for what they believe God has gifted them to do on earth for Him. It is also sad that some are being judged negatively because they received a comforting afterlife contact or sign from a loved one.

Some of the reasons for this modern-day condemnation given to me by good Christians, who are both for and against communicating with spirits, are these arguments:

Arguments Against Communicating with Spirits

- Translations of the Old Testament from the original Greek and Hebrew say we aren't allowed to call up or raise up the dead. Therefore, we aren't permitted to initiate the contact.
- The dead sleep until the Resurrection, therefore they aren't able to come and visit us before then.
- The body and soul stay in the grave until the Resurrection.
- The devil and demons are the *only* ones who can communicate with physical beings, so any and all spirits communicating with us must be from Satan.
- The spirit could come from God or from Satan, so to be on the safe side, we need to stay away from all spirits who are communicating with us, even the good ones, who are the informal saints.
- We don't want to offend God, or go against His will or our church.
- There is a chance that we will open ourselves up to demonic entities and possible possession if we start to communicate with the dead.

If people believe that the devil or demons are the *only* type of spirits who are able to communicate with us, they would understandably be frightened about these occurrences. Or if people believe that communicating with good spirits is too dangerous because the result would definitely be demonic attachments, attacks or possession, that would be another reason to steer clear of opening up any doors to the dark side by allowing communication with even good spirits or angels.

Others are concerned because they don't want to go against what they perceive to be God's commands in the Old Testament (Leviticus 19:31, Leviticus 20:27, Deuteronomy 18:10-13, 1 Chronicles 10:13-14, 2 Chronicles 33:6) which prohibit them from contacting or receiving afterlife signs even from good spirits. They desire to be faithful to what they've interpreted to be God's final Word on this matter. However, these particular Old Testament scriptures have left some Christians feeling confused because they believe the spirits, who they are communicating with, are their loved ones, and the encounters have brought them enormous peace and joy, as well as a closer relationship to God or Jesus. So they're torn and are looking for more answers and reassurances to resolve this conflict.

If any of the preceding describes your particular beliefs, but yet you have never personally researched the New Testament to learn if there is any information in there that exists that may give you a biblical green light to communicate with spirits and the way to do this safely, then your kneejerk reaction will, of course, be a negative one. If fear and condemnation are your automatic shutdown responses when you have been contacted by a deceased loved one, then you could be missing out on joy and consolation in your time of heartache and grief.

But what if interpretation, perceptions, and judgments are mistaken? For those of you who believe that God would never allow spirit communication and are frightened by it, I have some reassuring information to share with you below, which may never have been pointed out to you before. I ask that you at least read and consider the following information, which is taken from the New Testament of the Bible about spirit communication. It just might help to greatly alleviate some of your long-held fears and concerns about spiritual encounters.

Arguments For Communicating With Spirits

Followers of Jesus Christ are expected to emulate Christ's life and teachings as their role model, as documented in the New Testament. They are also expected to follow the teachings of Christ's closest disciples written about in the Bible. So it is worth noting that the New Testament does *not* mention that Jesus or His apostles have condemned communicating with spirits. In fact, just the opposite is recorded. The Bible confirms that Jesus and His disciples talked to spirits themselves! The New Testament of the Bible actually instructs us on how to carefully discern spirits, who we are communicating with, in 1 John 4:1-3, but doesn't prohibit or discourage it.

The Bible also shows us that souls do not literally sleep after they die. As an example, recorded in the New Testament, Jesus tells a parable about people who have died and were having a conversation with each other in the afterlife. The story is the Rich Man, Lazarus, and Abraham parable. In this narrative the Rich Man, who when on earth was unkind to the beggar Lazarus, had died and was now suffering torment in Hades. The Rich Man looks up and sees Abraham and the beggar Lazarus residing happily in the afterlife. The Rich Man pleads for Abraham to send Lazarus back to earth to warn his rich brothers to repent of their ways. Jesus conveyed that Abraham said that the brothers would not repent even if someone "rises from the dead" to warn them. Notice that Jesus did *not* say that it was impossible for Lazarus to return to earth to give them a warning though.

This parable can be read in full detail in Luke 16:19–31. But it indicates two things to me about spirits: (1) that the spirits of the Rich Man, Lazarus, and Abraham were not literally sleeping in the afterlife and were actually communicating with each other, and (2) that those who die realize that there is the possibility that spirits can be sent back to earth (rising from the dead) to communicate messages to human beings.

The Bible also says that in the Last Days, the Holy Spirit will be giving more gifts. Many theologians and scholars today believe that the signs we are now seeing in our world are pointing to those literal Last Days.

For your reflection and consideration, in the following I have paraphrased some scriptures from the New Testament of the Bible that I believe are accepting of the practice of spirit communication, especially because Christians are expected to live like Christ and His apostles. The scriptural references are included for your convenience so that you can look them up in your own Bible.

- Jesus, while living on earth, communicated with the spirits of Moses and Elijah on Mt. Tabor in front of His apostles Peter, James, and John. (Luke 9:28–36)
- Jesus said his followers would do greater things than the [miracle] works He did. (John 14:9–14)
- The Apostle Peter indicates that, in the Last Days, God said that He would pour out His Spirit on all people. Your sons

and daughters will prophesy, your young men will see visions, your old men will dream dreams. (Acts 2:17–18)
- The Apostle Paul indicates that the prophets, whom Paul was counseling, were talking to spirits, and that those spirits were under the control of the prophets. Paul referenced the fact that God is not a God of disorder but of peace when it comes to spirits. (1 Corinthians 14:26–33)
- The Apostle Paul lists gifts of the Holy Spirit such as, discerning of spirits, wisdom, knowledge, faith, healing, miraculous powers, and prophecy. (1 Corinthians 12:3–11)
- The Apostle John did not condemn communicating with spirits, but rather gave us instructions on how to test spirits to discern whether they are from God and could be believed. (1 John 4:1–3)

New Testament Superseding the Old Testament

So how does one reconcile the prohibitions in the Old Testament about spirit communication vs. the practice in the New Testament in which Jesus and His disciples were talking to spirits?

If you agree, as I do, that the New Testament of the Bible supersedes the Old Testament, and if you remember it states in the New Testament that the gifts of the Holy Spirit were given on Pentecost Sunday, and if you understand that the Apostle John in the New Testament was telling us how to responsibly test a spirit who we are communicating with, then I believe this helps solve your dilemma.

Did you notice that the Apostle Paul listed discerning of spirits as one of the gifts of the Holy Spirit? If Paul is to be believed, then when would one have the need to discern a spirit? When one was communicating with a spirit, of course!

Another example of the New Testament superseding some commands in the Old Testament would be the "eye for an eye" command being replaced with Jesus saying to "forgive your brother seventy times seven." And to love your brother as yourself. Therefore, do not the New Testament scriptures about spirit communication also show a new way too?

Safely Testing and Discerning Spirits

I do not believe that God would bless one with a spiritual gift and bestow afterlife contacts for His Divine Purposes, without giving us a way to protect ourselves too. I believe the problem comes into play when we do not use all the necessary discerning and protective armor that God has provided.

To communicate safely with spirits and angels that are around us but in other spiritual realms, it is imperative that one tests and discerns spirits, angels, and other holy beings as advised by John the Apostle.

Dear friends, do not believe every spirit, but test the spirits to see whether they are from God, because many false prophets have gone out into the world. This is how you can recognize the Spirit of God: Every spirit that acknowledges that Jesus Christ has come in the flesh is from God, but every spirit that does not acknowledge Jesus is not from God. This is the spirit of the antichrist, which you have heard is coming and even now is already in the world. (1 John 4:1–3).

3 Steps for Discernment and Protection

1. Ask the spirits if they acknowledge that Jesus Christ has come in the flesh.
2. Ask the spirits if they are committed and in service to Christ. They must answer yes.

3. Ask Jesus to bind and rebuke Satan and all his followers. Ask for the God-Christ's holy protection.

These steps are the keys to knowing if you are communicating with good spirits sent by God. The spirits who are not from God will leave for a temporary period of time, if you are faithful about taking these steps. This is especially important to do if a spirit is giving you messages. You want your messages to be truthful and not to be fooled or hurt by false messages. The Bible tells us that even Satan can disguise himself as an angel of light. And there are times that Satan will even have the audacity to disguise himself as Jesus. So only trust after verifying.

However, when we receive afterlife "signs" for our comfort, i.e., good dreams, rainbows, butterflies, coins etc. (as mentioned in the 20 Types of Afterlife Signs in Chapter 3) usually we do not have to worry about where these comforting "signs" are coming from. God allows these "signs" from our loved ones to help replace our heart's sorrow with His joy. These "signs" reassure us that our loved ones are safely in Heaven, as well as continuing to love, help, and gently guide us here on earth–until we meet again. As always, though, your source for truth on all things is God's Holy Spirit. Ask Him to speak directly to your heart on these matters.

* * *

AFTER-DEATH COMMUNICATIONS

* * *

AFTER-DEATH COMMUNICATIONS

CHAPTER 3

20 Types of Afterlife Signs & Tips

> [Jesus said] "Do not let your hearts be troubled. Trust in God; trust also in me. In my Father's house are many rooms; if it were not so, I would have told you. I am going there to prepare a place for you. And if I go and prepare a place for you, I will come back and take you to be with me that you also may be where I am." (John 14:1-3).

Listed below are of some of the myriad of ways our Prayer Wave For After-Death Communication group have received after-death communications and signs (ADCs) from Jesus, angels and our loved ones. Some of these ways are certainly blockbusters, but many are subtle yet still extremely valid, meaningful, and cherished by us. May this help you to recognize your own personal ADC gifts from God.

1. Dream Visits:

Dreams that are vivid and comforting, in which you feel you are actually talking on the phone to or visiting with your loved one or pet, or that they are in the room, even if you cannot see them. It is important to know, however, that if the dream did *not* comfort you, even if someone looked like your loved one was in the dream, this was not an ADC from them.

The operative word is "comforting," for God sends ADCs from our loved ones for the purpose of comforting us. Not to cause us anxiety or fear. If you are receiving disturbing dream visits from your loved one, be sure to ask for God's protection before you go to sleep every night. This has proven to shift those upsetting dreams to the comforting ones we all desire.

2. Visual Appearances:

Seeing an apparition of a loved one or a deceased pet in the room, or in your mind's eye, either while you are fully awake or in a twilight state of sleep. You may see only their face or a partial or full body appearance. They may look transparent, semitransparent or solid in form. They may appear in color, black and white, appearing like silhouettes, or looking like a photograph or a movie clip. You may see symbols, printed messages or objects. Your eyes could be opened or closed when seeing something in your mind's eye.

Seeing someone who looks just like your loved one when you have been thinking about them and needing a sign from them. Seeing the face of your loved briefly appear on another person's face.

Seeing a loved one appear in the mirror or in a window, or handprints or messages appearing in a steamy shower.

Seeing in the dark—with your eyes open—brilliant white light; forms that float by you resembling white or colored cloud-like mists; or twinkling lights— yet you don't have an eye problem.

Seeing in the daylight—with your eyes open—what looks like transparent, amoeba-shaped forms floating by you; seeing cloud-like mists in white or color; or seeing a brilliant white light—yet you don't have an eye problem.

Children have a God-given gift to see and hear spirits. Please believe them. (I write about children's gifts in *Heaven Talks To Children: Afterlife Contacts, Spiritual Gifts and Loving Messages.*)

3. Pets:

Your pet may be looking, staring, barking or meowing and getting excited at something in the room that only they can see. Pets not only see spirits, but our pets will often come back from Heaven to visit us. They may visit in a dream or in your twilight state. You may hear a sound they used to make. Something that they used to play with may move on its own. You may smell their scent around you.

4. Audio and Music:

Hearing your loved one's voice or sounds that connect you to them. This could be heard internally inside of your head, or externally in the room.

Songs on the radio, or played by a DJ or a band that are meaningful to your loved one and to you, especially when you have just been thinking about your loved one.

A song that connects you to your loved one that you have heard recently, but it continually plays in your head numerous times during the day.

A song playing in your mind, that you have not heard recently, that connects you to your loved one. You may even find yourself humming it before you realize what is happening.

Morse code type of sounds being tapped in your ear–yet you don't have a hearing problem.

Although this is rare, there is a story in this book where someone else's voice suddenly and spontaneously speaks through the woman's mouth in order to get your immediate and urgent attention to keep her from harm.

5. Telepathic Thoughts:

You may hear your own voice speaking in your head, but it is not your own thoughts. They are separate from what you have been thinking about. These thoughts are very strong and may be repeated for emphasis so that you will notice. This often happens after praying for guidance.

6. Scents:

Scents that are unexplained as to how the scent or aroma got into the room. It may smell like your loved one or have the scent of something they used, e.g., their cologne, cigar smoke, cigarettes, or baking aroma. It may also be an overwhelmingly pleasant smell that surrounds you and seems to come out of nowhere, e.g. floral scents.

7. Touches:

Touches that are ticklish, quivering or a pressure type of a feeling on your face, nose, lips, hand or arm. You may feel like you want to scratch that strong ticklish feeling. Many times these are what we affectionately refer to as "spirit kisses." You may feel a hug. Feeling a hand on your shoulder or someone holding your hand. You may even feel your head being massaged or patted, or your hair being stroked. Some people set up a communication code of "yes" or "no" this way. Some people know which loved one is communicating with them by the different areas the spirits will consistently touch. For example, your father may touch the top of your head, while your mother may touch your arm, if you have requested this.

8. Presence:

Sensing or feeling a spiritual, strong or heavy energy presence in the room. Sometimes your ears will close up when you feel this strong energy presence.

Feeling a breeze going by you or a coolness around you in a closed room. Feeling a strong and sustaining chill going deeply all through you while thinking of your loved one. The feeling gives you a great feeling of peace and calm and is different in intensity than the chills you get when you are cold.

Sensing a warm, wonderful feeling of love and peace go all through you.

Feeling like an electrical sensation has just gone through you.

Sensing weight on your bed, as if someone came and sat or laid down beside you.

Waking up at the exact time on your clock that your loved one has passed is caused by a spirit presence.

9. Electrical Manipulations:

Lights, touch lamps, street lamps, garage doors, fans, TVs and radios etc. going on and off by themselves. The TV automatically channel surfing or choosing a specific station. A clock stopping at a significant hour that has meaning to you. Video game controllers taking over the screen.

10. Computers:

Music and pictures being downloaded on their own or

showing up on your screen. Emails showing to be sent by you, however, you did not send it, nor did anyone else in the house. Screen names showing up of your loved one, when no one has been using that screen name or the computer. Computer programs turning on by itself. Video games being played or turning on by itself.

11. Phones, Texts, Caller ID:

You may hear static on the phone instead of a voice. Receiving calls from disconnected phone numbers showing on the caller ID, yet there is no logical or natural explanation.

Messages from your loved one being left on your answering machine or voice mail.

Old or new text messages showing up on your cell phone from your loved one.

12. Objects:

Objects being moved, left out in the open, disappearing, and reappearing on their own when no one was around. The object may connect you to your loved one. Even if it doesn't, you realize there's no way the event could happen without unseen help. This also would include letters, notes and cards.

Objects you "happen" to find while shopping, or on the ground, that connect you to a loved one. Or the found object is something that you have been wanting or seeking and almost miraculously came upon when you needed a pick-me-up.

13. Feathers and Gifts:

Finding feathers repeatedly, as if they were left just for you.

Receiving an unexpected gift that the bearer had no idea has special meaning to you. A gift (or your favorite color of flowers) may also arrive on a significant date to show you that your loved one remembered it too.

14. Coins:

Coins mysteriously appearing. The same coin denomination may be repeated over time. For instance, it may be only pennies that appear for you. Sometimes a coin will have a significant year embossed on it.

15. Photos:

Photos or pictures mysteriously left out for you to see. Framed pictures being crooked, falling off the wall or falling over flat on a table, of your loved one, when no one was around to have caused this to happen.

White misty forms appearing in photos, sometimes referred to as orbs. These are considered to be spirits showing that they were there.

16. Birds, Animals, Butterflies, Dragonflies, Insects:

A butterfly, dragonfly, animal, bird or any insect that seem to know you or act like they belong to you, or act peculiar. They can be anywhere from just one to hundreds of them when they are around you.

17. Rainbows, Shooting Stars, Clouds:

Rainbows that appear after you have asked for a sign from your loved one, or on a significant date. It may be sunny and clear one minute and then some clouds and moisture may suddenly form in order to produce that gorgeous rainbow for you. A shooting star that suddenly appears in the sky when you are thinking about your loved one. Cloud formations that appear to be your loved one's face, an angel or other meaningful figures in the clouds.

18. Numbers, Names, License Plates, Receipts:

Numbers, names and messages that have significance to you on things like license plates, sales receipts, signs, or checks. It may be your loved one's birth date or date of passing. Your loved one's name may show up on a receipt or is the name of the person waiting on you.

19. Candles:

Candles flickering wildly as if someone was trying to wave "hi" to you through the candle. Candles being lit by themselves.

20. Godincidences:

Many of the signs we receive from our loved ones will seem like amazingly lucky and meaningful coincidences, or synchronicities, but from my experiences and countless others who I have interviewed, I believe these coincidences are really orchestrated from above. We like to refer to them as Godincidences. I feel very strongly that these Godincidences are blessings from God, through our loved ones to us, who are constantly watching over and praying for us. If your mind suggests to you that this is "such an amazing coincidence," then please realize you have been blessed and are very lovingly being cared for by God from the heavens, through your loved ones and angels.

Helpful Tips for Receiving an ADC

Tip #1 – Dream Visits

Dreams are one the easiest way for spirits to visit us, because our dream state can open up a spiritual doorway for spirits to communicate with us.

1. Ask God every night to allow your loved one to visit you in a comforting dream.

2. Very important—ask for God (or Jesus') holy protection before you sleep or meditate so that your experiences will be comforting ones.

3. Ask God to allow you to remember your dream visit.

4. Keep a pad and pen nearby or under your pillow to record your dream before you are fully awake, so you won't forget it by the time you have completely awoken.

5. Visualize yourself with your loved one in pleasant and happy surroundings, talking to them about things that you have been wanting to tell them, as you fall off to sleep.

6. It is much easier for our loved ones to get through to us when we are feeling peaceful. Please pray to God to help you feel His peace in your heart at this time of your life when you most need it. Ask God to replace your heart's sorrow with His joy. God is your best friend. He loves you completely, and He wants to heal and comfort your heart.

7. Be patient in waiting for God to answer, and trust that He will, for your prayers have gone straight to God's loving heart. This will help you relax about getting a dream visit.

8. Ask others to pray for you too. Group prayers are very powerful. We would be happy to pray for you if you join our private Facebook group called After Death Communications and Prayer Wave.

Facebook.com/groups/Afterdeathcommunicationsprayerwave

9. Remember, it is only a true spiritual visit from a loved one in a dream, if the dream is a comforting experience. If you are getting dreams that are causing you distress, wherein your loved one looks to be in pain, lost, ignoring you, angry at you, or causing you hurt feelings by being affectionate to another person, and rejecting you, etc. This is not your loved one in the dream. God sends our loved ones to us for the purpose of bringing us peace and comfort! To help stop getting these kinds of distressful and hurtful dreams, please be sure to faithfully say your protection prayers to God every night before you go to sleep.

Tip #2 – Meditation and Prayer

Meditation and prayer can put us into a tranquil twilight state that can open a doorway for spiritual communication. Soft music is a soothing way to get you into a relaxed state for meditation, as well as guided meditation tapes. I have created a guided meditation tape called "Meditation of God's Love and Healing: For Those Who Grieve" in which you can spend time with your loved one or angel. To order, please visit www.christineduminiak.com. Before you begin meditating it is very important to ask for God or Jesus' protection, because you only want the good spirits from God to visit you.

Tip #3 – Specific Request

Say a prayer to God to allow your loved one to visit you in a comforting way.

Then state a specific type of ADC to your loved one that you would recognize as a sign from them, e.g. a butterfly. This way you will be able to definitely recognize and claim your ADC when you receive it. Please be patient while waiting for your request to be acknowledged. Don't feel discouraged. Sometimes our loved ones are on important missions for God and will wait until their missions are completed before giving us signs again. Also, they have to learn how to communicate using spirit energy now, since they no longer have physical bodies.

Tip #4 – Gratitude

It is helpful and encouraging for the spirit of your loved one if you acknowledge them in some way when you have received an ADC from them. A simple "Thank you," would be very appreciated by them, for they hear everything you say to them. Let God know, too, how much you appreciate His kindness to you, since spirits can only give us signs with God's permission. Expressing gratitude may bring you more blessings.

Tip #5 – Repeated Patterns

Once you start to notice how your loved one is contacting you, they will usually repeat the same pattern, so you will more easily be able to recognize their special visits. After you recognize their particular signs on a consistent basis, they may start to branch out into different styles of communications. They like to show you how well they are progressing in their communications skills!

Tip #6 – Simultaneous thought

When you receive an ADC, you may also get a simultaneous thought or knowingness that you have just received a sign. That is because our loved ones will put thoughts into our minds so that we will know the sign is from them. Sometimes you will feel an overpowering feeling of love attached to the ADC.

Tip #7 – Claim it

Most ADCs are subtle. If your first thought is, "I just received a sign," then go with that feeling. Don't over-analyze it or second-guess it. Just enjoy it! Your first impression is usually the correct one. Our loved ones dearly want us to know they are with us by giving us "signs." So honor them my simply accepting it and not rejecting it. If you have to err on whether or not it truly was a sign, err on the positive!

Tip #8 – Feeling peaceful

It is helpful to be at peace with your loved one's returning Home to God, in order to be better able to receive a comforting communication. Feeling peaceful is an emotion that is very hard to experience when you are, understandably, very upset and hurting as you go through the grieving process. But being emotionally overwrought can give out negative energy, thus, making it harder for your loved one to get through to you, or for you to even notice a sign from them. However, all things are possible with God, and He may bless you with an after-death communication, no matter what the circumstances, because He wants to comfort you and bring you peace. Pray for peace for your anguished heart. Pray for acceptance and comfort, so that you can go on with your life contented in knowing that you will be fully reunited once again.

* * *

PART II
After-Death Communication Stories

CHAPTER 4

Visits From Jesus Christ

The Lord is close to the brokenhearted and saves those who are crushed in spirit (Psalm 34:18).

Jesus Spoke to Me

When the Prayer Wave For After-Death Communication group first started, I joined as one of its first members. Two days later I had something incredibly wonderful happen to me. Some would call it a religious experience, others would call it an out of body experience. Whatever you want to call it, it was Divine, in my eyes. My experience was this:

I was quietly relaxing, but definitely not dreaming, and I seemed to be suddenly transported to my daughter's house, which is about fifty miles from where I live. I was in the presence of my daughter and her daughter. They both left to go into her bedroom to look at something or other. I suddenly heard a deep masculine voice speaking. I knew there were no men in the house at that time, so I walked back to the area where the voice came from to investigate what was going on! Now, strangely, my daughter and granddaughter were no longer there! As I looked around I saw no one, but the voice continued to speak, and I knew it was speaking to me.

I listened closely, but it seemed like I could not quite hear what was being said to me. So I said aloud, that I couldn't hear him. So the voice got louder, but for some reason, its tone dropped lower again. This happened two or three times. But what I did hear loud and clear, I shall always remember; I heard the voice state, "I AM GOD, THE CHRIST."

This was so incredible to me! It was such a beautiful experience. I must reiterate that this was not a dream. I have had several such experiences and I do know the difference! This is something I will never forget!

ELAINE STEGALL

Jesus' Army

Two days after I felt inspired by who I believe was the Holy Spirit to form the Internet group called Prayer Wave For After-Death Communication in September 2000, I was lying in bed praying before I went off to sleep. Suddenly I saw a vision of a beautiful man's face. His hair was brown and shoulder length. He had a beard and a mustache—similar to the paintings of Jesus. He had the most exquisite eyes that looked as transparent as glass. The eyes were so outstanding; they were definitely not of this physical world. I recognized this face to be the face of Jesus Christ.

As I watched, stunned and amazed, I was shown a second vision of Jesus, but this time He was smiling, wearing an Army cap on His head, and holding a pair of binoculars over his eyes—all the while Jesus was looking downward towards Earth through those binoculars.

I understood instinctively that Jesus was conveying the message that He was watching over our newly formed Prayer Wave For After-Death Communication Internet group from

Heaven, and that I was part of His Army. I felt His pleasure and blessings towards our group and our mission. Our mission is to pray to our one Creator for each other in our group (as well as for others who ask) to request His blessings of a loving and comforting after-death communication or sign from our loved ones in spirit, who are now back Home with Him.

I will carry the image of this sacred visit from Jesus Christ forever in my mind and heart.

Jesus and Our Heavenly Father have been blessing our "Prayer Wave For After-Death Communication" group since 2000 with many tender, loving contacts from our loved ones in Heaven in order to bring us joy, comfort, and healing. Prayer really does touch God's heart.

CHRISTINE MARIE DUMINIAK

Jesus Said I Have Nothing To Fear

I am a Christian and for a while I had been struggling with some spiritual issues. I have always questioned the sacrifice made by Jesus when He died on the cross. "Why did he have to die," I asked, "and how does his death wipe out the sins of mankind?" I have struggled with this basic concept of Christianity. I always felt like I wasn't a "real" Christian because I didn't have an answer.

I decided to pray and meditate about this. During this meditation I found myself transported to a bench near a peaceful pond. A person dressed in white robes came up and sat down beside me. He was Jesus! He told me that, as a mystery of God's, a sacrifice was necessary for something good to happen. He said that He was born to save mankind, and that the ultimate sacrifice was necessary to wipe out man's sins—for the Son of God to die for mankind.

Upon hearing these words, from our Lord and Savior, I immediately knew the truth of what He was saying to me, and tears came to my eyes. Because of this blessed and humbling visit to me, I was instantaneously relieved of this unnecessary burden I had been carrying for such a long, long time. I finally knew that I, too, was a very loved follower of Jesus Christ.

Some weeks later, I started to wonder if this incredible visit from Jesus was just a product of wishful thinking or an overactive imagination, but during another time while praying and meditating, I had a second visit from Jesus. During this visit from Jesus He said to me, "I am with you and you have nothing to fear."

I did not tell anyone about this second visit from Jesus. But an opportunity presented itself when I had a chance to ask Sunni Welles, a well-known Christian woman who has been gifted to be able to communicate with her angels and other good spirits. I only asked her if Jesus Christ did indeed visit me. Ms. Welles checked with her angels and they said to tell me, "Larry, yes, Christ did speak to you. He said that He is with you and that you have nothing to fear."

Unbeknownst to Ms. Welles, these were the same words Jesus spoke to me during His second visit to me! I knew then, that Jesus had truly blessed me with a personal visit.

LARRY

Jesus and My Papa Angel

My dear Papa Angel returned Home to God a few years ago, and I've missed him more than I can say. Since my dad's passing, I have received numerous after-death communication signs from him including songs, butterflies, birds, and more. Lately, I had been fervently praying that I would be able to meet Jesus and get to talk to Him too. One night, after I made this prayer request, I dreamed that I was in the company of an old man; he was very worn, torn and ragged. He was so very tattered and tired that I was worried about him and his welfare. I kept talking to him to see if I could help him in some way. After a short while, this very tired, old man suddenly transformed himself and he was now young, strong, healthy and very, very handsome.

This very handsome young man was now wearing a dark brown robe and brown sandals on his feet. His hair was dark and long and he had a beard. His eyes were the most beautiful brown eyes I have ever seen—other than my dad's, whose eyes were so beautiful and I felt were the mirrors to his beautiful soul. I just stared at this handsome man in amazement, wondering who was he? Then I suddenly realized and screamed out loud, "You're Jesus!" With that, Jesus just looked at me and smiled so lovingly at me. He radiated pure love, and he just glowed all over from head to toe!

To make the dream even more meaningful, my precious dad was in this dream too. Although I couldn't see him, I could hear his voice. He was telling me that he was with God and he was very, very happy. Jesus smiled at me and confirmed that this was indeed true; that I should never worry about my dad again or ever feel sad for him because he was eternally happy.

I will never forget the radiant smile on Jesus' face. Jesus' voice was so full of love and compassion, that I immediately felt safe and extremely happy. I knew from Jesus' blessed visit to me that I did not have to worry about my dad's welfare; that he was with Jesus and he was in Paradise.

LAURA HAYES

The Baby Jesus

After sixteen years of marriage, my husband decided he no longer wanted to be married to me. I was devastated. Strangely I started seeing, in my mind's eye, a little infant with a crown on his head. I had no idea who this infant was, so I asked our priest Father Paul about it. After describing what I saw, Father Paul said I was being shown the Infant of Prague (the baby Jesus).

Eventually my husband and I got back together, and I realized that the Infant of Prague was appearing to me to let me know that everything was going to be all right.

Two months later, a "Godincidence" occurred. My nephew was killed, and I ordered a mass card from the Franciscan Order of Priests for masses to be said for my nephew. The Franciscans sent me back a mass card that had a Novena Prayer to the Infant of Prague!

I talk to God a lot and ask Him a lot of questions. If my answer from God is to be a "Yes," the Infant of Prague appears. If the answer is "No," I see the full body of the Lord in tears.

LINDA MARIE

Jesus and My Shadow

For weeks I had been praying to Jesus to please hold my beloved dog Shadow. I asked Jesus to tell him he is special and how much I love him and miss him. I asked Jesus to pet and kiss his little head and to reassure Shadow that he is all right now. I was so afraid that Shadow didn't understand what happened to him when he passed over.

One day after again saying my prayer, and while I was driving, I saw a vision of Jesus. Jesus was standing with his back towards me. He had beautiful brown hair, which was wavy and it hung a little below his shoulders. Jesus had a brown mustache and a beard. He was standing very close to me. I could see his upper back all the way to the top of His head. Even though His back was facing me, I could still see the side of His holy wonderful face. Jesus was in a white robe and holding my little dog Shadow. Shadow's fur looked very, very white, like it did after one of his baths. Right behind Jesus and Shadow there was a bluish cast, and a little farther beyond, there was a white, foggy cloud-like area.

Dear, sweet Jesus was holding Shadow in His arms and was petting him. He was smiling and looking down at my little dog. The love Jesus had for Shadow just glowed from Him, and I heard Him say how much He loves Shadow. The love I saw in Shadow's eyes as he looked up at Jesus' face told me he understood that he was very loved and that he was now okay. I could tell that Shadow understood that this was a very special visit by the look I saw in his eyes.

It all was so wonderful and truly beautiful. My baby looked so content and so trusting of the Lord. I am so relieved, happy, and so very blessed to have had my prayers answered in this most profound way.

KATHY F.

* * *

AFTER-DEATH COMMUNICATIONS

* * *

CHAPTER 5

Angels

God has assigned angels to each one of us to help guide and protect us here on earth. Here are a few stories demonstrating how God's holy angels work on our behalf.

The Angel And The Spider

On June 5, 1997, I had a very odd yet wondrous experience happen. I am a landscape contractor and was going to load up my truck with mulch like I do every day. But on that day I felt very ill, almost unbearably so. It was 10 a.m. and I decided to drive myself to the hospital. When I arrived at the hospital's emergency room around 11 a.m., I actually passed out.

Eventually I was diagnosed and being treated for Rocky Mountain spotted fever, but the treatment was not working. I had four doctors and plenty of medical staff by my side, including an orthopedic surgeon who had to explain the real possibility of having to remove my left leg up to my hip. A specialist from a prestigious university hospital's Disease & Poison Center came and did a culture. Results showed I had been bitten by a poisonous brown recluse spider. The poison was traveling up my leg at a very rapid rate, starting from below my left kneecap, where the bite originated. The race was now on to change the medicine that would intravenously enter my body and fight for my life, not just my leg.

After being resuscitated three separate times after my heart and body shut down, the medical staff was barely able to keep me going. At one point they told my wife to call a priest because I was not responding to anything.

Now comes the strange mystery that took place. The hospital staff couldn't do any more than they were already doing for me. With the hospital staff's combined one hundred years of medical experience, plus their spending all day working on me, by 11 p.m. that same night I was put into a Critical Care Room. I had round-the-clock supervision by the staff. The nurse taking care of me from 11 p.m. till 6 a.m. the next morning identified herself as Carol.

Carol told me she had three kids and a dog, but what I remember most of all about her was her long, shaggy, big, and bushy blonde hairdo. She said she had just turned thirty years old. Carol took very good care of me. I would say too good! She emphatically said, "Dan, you must be bathed four times tonight, shaved twice, get your feet washed six times, your fingernails trimmed, and your hair needs washing too. Plus, your temperature and pulse have to be taken twelve times. We can't let the bacteria give you an infection or it could kill you."

I pleaded with Carol, "Please may I just get some sleep, it's just too much for me. I haven't gotten any rest since I got here at 11 a.m. yesterday morning." Carol replied, "Oh no, we must do these things. No rest yet, Dan! Turn over to the other side now so I can wash you. Okay?"

By 5 a.m. I had convinced myself that Carol, my blonde nurse, was out to get me. So I decided to wait to complain to the first person who came into my room after Carol finished her shift. At about 6:45 a.m. the specialist from the university's hospital entered my room. He said he stayed all night at the hospital, as my case had him very concerned. He said that only nine out of twenty-nine patients bitten by the brown recluse spider had survived in the five-state area that year.

I took this opportunity to plead with the specialist, asking if I may please get some rest because Carol, the blonde-headed nurse who took care of me all night, wouldn't let me get one minute of sleep the whole time. I also asked the doctor if I could request another nurse tonight, so I could finally get some much needed rest and sleep.

The specialist said, "OK, Daniel, I'll check at the nurse's station and find out what went on and I'll be right back." Ten minutes later the specialist came back into my room with shocking news, "Daniel, the nurse guarding you last night did not have a long, shaggy blonde hairdo; she was not thirty years old with three kids and a dog. Actually, the nurse who took care of you had short gray hair, was sixty-two, and had no children. And if you look in the mirror here, you'll find that you weren't shaved at all, and you aren't as clean as you thought! I believe, Daniel, your friend Carol was your guardian angel, and she kept you from sleeping to keep you alive. You see, if you had fallen asleep, the chances of your being alive today would have been very low."

I thank God for Carol.

DAN BANGERT

My Blue Angel

Dreams have been a natural way of my receiving spiritual communication, sometimes even premonitions of things to come. When I would receive a dream that had a specific color of blue in it, which I refer to as angel-blue, it has been a signal to me that my dream has special spiritual significance.

I would like to share a very significant dream that was life-altering for me that occurred on my birthday. I dreamt that I was back in the town where I grew up. I was just sort of wandering around downtown, but this place was different than I had remembered. It was as if I had gone back in time in this very town. I went inside a building that seemed unfamiliar to me once I got inside. I came across a lady with blonde hair who looked strikingly familiar.

She was the one and only person I saw in my dream. We were talking about nothing in particular, and I told her I had to go. As I walked outside she called my name. I turned around and she said, "God loves you." I was stunned. This message came out of nowhere. I said to her, "God is my best friend." She just smiled and nodded in affirmation.

I got into a car and sat behind the wheel. I was the only one in the car, except on the passenger's seat was a live blue rabbit! An angel-blue-colored rabbit! This color was the deepest, most angelic shade of blue that you could ever have imagined, and this is the same angel-blue color that I have received in other dreams that have been significant spiritual events for me.

This blue rabbit hopped up into my lap, and I started driving downtown. I was stroking its fur and marveling at the sight of a blue rabbit in my lap!

It was then that it hit me!

The lady I met was my spirit guide Sarah. The reason I know her name was Sarah is this. I had asked God in my prayers one night, many months ago, to introduce me to my spirit guide. After my prayers were finished, I had just begun to fall off to sleep and in my ear I heard the name "Sarah" whispered very softly. I sat straight up in bed and said, "Sarah?" and then I heard it again!

The reason I knew I had met Sarah, my spirit guide, in my dream with the blue rabbit was this—the woman looked just like my aunt, whose name is Sarah! So by my spirit guide's appearing to me in my dream looking like my aunt, it was her way of letting me know who she was and also her name.

This was a life-changing event for me. I've done things when I was younger that I am not proud of, downright ashamed of, and I have wondered for the longest time if God would ever forgive me for those things. That shame and remorse has kept me from loving myself and has contributed to my low self- esteem.

Now because Sarah, my spirit guide, gave me the message that God loves me, I feel like I can start to love myself. I mean if God loves me, then surely I must be worthy of love! And to have that type of dream happen on my birthday just makes it all the more special!

With love, hope, prayer, and peace,

K. MICHELLE

The Angel in the Ocean

It was Father's Day in June of 1996, and. I was visiting my friends in North Carolina. They had just moved down there from Northeastern Pennsylvania. It was a very windy day and the ocean was very rough. My friend's mom had advised us not to go out into the water that day, but like all rebellious children in our thirties, we did our own thing.

It began as a great time, frolicking like two children jumping the waves. Suddenly, I was in the clutches of a powerful undertow and lost my glasses. I was being taken farther and farther away from shore and screaming frantically for help. Soon I was in a horrendous whirlpool going helplessly round and round, like limp clothes in the spin cycle of a washing machine. I was not only dizzy but also blind-as-a-bat without my glasses. I could not even see which way the shoreline was to attempt to swim to safety, even if I could have been able to somehow miraculously free myself. However, I did briefly catch sight of one of my friends waving and crying helplessly, "I can't help you, Kimmie."

I was wearing a crucifix ring and felt it slipping ever so slowly off of my finger. Everything seemed to be in slow motion now. It seemed like the longest finger in the world, yet I had no strength to even attempt to rescue my ring. However, I was totally aware of its inching off. By this time I had pretty much given myself over to God and thought, "Well if this is how You want me to die . . . ." No sooner had I surrendered myself when I saw my loving dad—who had passed over eight years earlier from cancer. He looked happy and healthy now, which was very different from the last time I saw him on earth.

Seconds later, after getting a glimpse of my dad's spirit, I saw what I now fully realize was my guardian angel. I saw coral lips, light hair, and ivory, almost transparent, skin. There were no eyes visible or nose that I recall, but the other three features were very clear and vividly colored.

It was only seconds following these two apparitions that something lifted me out of the water and literally placed me in the arms of my friend. I believe I was truly lifted up on angel's wings. I was given CPR after passing out and only two hours later I was eating at Chi-Chi's Restaurant!

Afterwards, we found out that the area we were swimming in was off-limits because there were no lifeguards nearby, but on that day— Father's Day—I had the Divine Lifeguard watching over me.

KIM S. MANGAN

* * *

AFTER-DEATH COMMUNICATIONS

* * *

CHAPTER 6

Audio: Voices, Music & Sounds

> Voices, music, and sounds transmitted to us by loved ones, can be heard either inside of our minds or outside of ourselves. Meaningful songs that happen to come on the radio, TV, etc., frequently are ADCs.

Dara's Heart Light

As a teenager I worked with disabled kids for many years, and several times I had premonitions about their health. As a nurse today, I have that sixth sense that nurses get when a patient is going to die, but I no longer have or am attuned to the premonitions of the past. Something I do miss.

When I was fifteen years old I was hired to be one of the first parental relief workers for parents of disabled kids. I lived with one of the families on weekends, helped around their house, and looked after their child. Hence I was given the privilege of being part of the life of their little girl Dara. Dara was eighteen months old when I met her. A tumor had been removed from her brain stem, subsequently requiring a trach (breathing tube in her throat) and a tube in her belly to eat.

I don't know if anyone remembers the old Drowsy Dolls, but that was my first image of Dara. I fell in love with her immediately. Her blonde hair was all shaved up the back, and she was wearing pink pajamas. I took her upstairs that first night, and she had a choking spell and turned blue on me. As a young teenager, seeing this happen really frightened me, yet, I knew I was going to have to deal with Dara's seizures and medical condition if I was going to be of any help to the family. So I made her parents give Dara to me to hold immediately after this spell. I knew, if I didn't hold her right away, I would never get over my fear.

I lived with Dara and her family on weekends for almost two years. I was Dara's "Jenny," and she was just a joy. She smiled and laughed at anything I did with her. Sadly, Dara died suddenly in November of 1983, when the tumor took over. A tumor that was almost undetectable in June. I had a premonition that something was wrong during the last two days she was ill, even though it wasn't apparent to others. She died in her mom's arms. A yellow rose from me, roses from her sister, and Dara's doll were all laid with her as she was being prepared for her spiritual Home.

The family had moved two weeks before Dara died. About four months later, I was at their new home visiting her bereaved parents. It was a very quiet morning. No one was up and I was standing still at the window watching the sunrise. Across the room were several of Dara's old toys and stuffed animals. Suddenly, the "heart bear" lit its "heart light" and played three notes. At the same time in my head I heard these precious words, "I love you." ADC or imagination? I believe an ADC. There were NO BATTERIES in the bear, and there was no movement in the room.

Dara's family encouraged me to try and get into nursing, something I never thought I could ever do. I am now a nurse because of Dara. Eighteen years later I still have Dara's stethoscope with me and believe Dara looks over me. Between us there is one veil, obscured from one side but transparent from the other.

JENNY

Loving and Forgiving

A day after my mother passed over in 2004 my sisters and I met with the funeral director. One of our tasks was having to choose four hymns for our mom's funeral mass. My sisters and I knew three hymns that our mother definitely liked, but we were stumped concerning the fourth one. We just didn't know. Our mother obviously knew of our hymn dilemma and took care of the problem that very same evening. While I was lying in bed, I heard the lyrics to a hymn being played very strongly in my mind. They were, "Loving and forgiving are You, oh Lord. Slow to anger, rich in kindness, loving and forgiving are You."

I was stunned, but delighted! My dear mom had come back from Heaven to choose her fourth funeral hymn! Although I hadn't been very familiar with this particular hymn, I of course went with it. The next day I called the funeral director and requested it.

I also believe my mother was delivering another type of message to me about God through this hymn. I believe she wanted to share with me how loving and forgiving God is—now that she had personally met Him. This was very significant for me, because I had grown up being educated by strict Catholic nuns who seemed to mainly dwell on God's anger at us, instead of His love. My mother wanted to pass on the important message of God's love and forgiveness.

Over the years, my mother has given me a heads-up in Church whenever "Loving and Forgiving" was going to be played at mass. I would feel her tickling the left side of my nose, which is the area my mother has consistently chosen to touch to let me know when she is around. I can't tell you how comforting all of this has been to me. I am so very, very grateful to God and my mom.

CHRISTINE DUMINIAK

Beaming Me Up

In October 1998, a special person in my life died. Rod was a dear friend and an "adopted" second father to me. We had become closer after my own father passed away in 1994, and now I had lost him as well.

I had no idea that he had been sick with cancer because it had been his wish that no one knew. So when he died, I was devastated. My whole world was turned upside down, and the floor of my world went out from under me, leaving me with nothing to hold onto. The hole in my life was as deep and dark as the grief that consumed my heart. I was inconsolable and I thought that nothing in my life would ever be right again.

A few days after my friend's death, I started praying to God for a sign to let me know that he was all right. I felt that if I knew that Rod was all right, then I would be all right. I had never prayed like that before. This was not the nice little prayers of childhood. This was the gut-wrenching, sobbing, on-the-floor, and on-your-knees type of praying. Actually, it was more like pleading than praying. I didn't have long to wait for an answer though.

About three days after my prayer, I got my answer. I'm an RN and was working at our local hospital, doing my usual night shift. It was a quiet night, and I had just finished doing first rounds and checking on everyone. It was around 2 a.m. and I had just sat down at the nurses' station to start my charting. I was alone at the time at the desk, as my aide had gone down the hall to answer a patient's call light. That's when "things" started to happen.

As I sat writing, I gradually became aware of a lovely feeling of happiness surrounding me. I was very much aware that this feeling was coming to me from somewhere; it was definitely not coming from me. This feeling of total happiness and pure joy slowly grew and grew, until it finally crested like a wave and washed over me. It was delicious! As I basked in this feeling, I became aware of Rod's presence standing next to me. It was the same feeling you get when someone comes into the room you are in, and even though you haven't turned to look at them; you still know they are there. Then I "heard" Rod's voice, not with my ears but in my head, and quite clearly! This had never happened to me before, but I wasn't afraid; it seemed like the most natural thing in the world.

He was gently scolding me, using his most matter-of-fact voice, the one he used when he didn't like something I was doing. He said, "Now, Jan, don't be silly! I'm okay! I'm FINE! (The emphasis was on FINE!) Please, no more sadness, no more tears. I know you care." And then he was gone, leaving me with a glorious feeling of joy! In fact, that feeling stayed with me for a long time, gradually diminishing, and leaving me with great peace of mind, knowing that my beloved friend was just fine, and that I would see him again someday.

I knew God had given me the answer to my prayer!

JANET

These Boots Are Made For Walkin'

In 2000, three months after my dad returned back Home

to God, my mother, sister, and I traveled west to Arizona to visit my lovely cousin Jeanne. We had hoped the vacation would be a happy diversion and something fun to take our minds off of our loss, and we weren't disappointed! My cousin and her husband were the perfect hosts and so very thoughtful.

We were constantly talking about Daddy during the trip and I had many ADCs from him while in AZ. These included a fly, a humming bird, and a butterfly that followed me all around a Catholic gift shop. However, the one ADC that was the most sensational had to do with a song.

One evening, while still in Arizona, we all gathered around and watched old 8-mm home movies. My dad was in those movies as was one of my younger cousins, who happened to be wearing white go-go boots. We loved getting to see my dad again this way, and also got a big kick out of those white go-go boots. I even made the remark, "Wow, would you look at those go-go boots!" And we laughed watching the fashion styles from the 1960s.

During the middle of the night, when I was in that twilight state of consciousness, I began to hear a song being played in my head. The song was Nancy Sinatra's "These Boots Are Made for Walkin." I couldn't believe what I was hearing, and I was thrilled. This song meant that my dad had been there with us enjoying those old home movies too; it meant he heard my remark about those go- go boots! What an announcement of his presence! But that song ADC didn't stop there.

The next morning we boarded a plane to go back home. I was silently talking to my dad asking him to let us know in some way that he was with us because my mother, his wife of almost sixty years, felt very lonely and was especially missing him so.

I had on a pair of headphones that were plugged into the airplane's radio console. My mom was plugged in also and was having a hard time understanding how to work the radio dials. I was trying to help her find a good station, when the ADC happened!

I heard in my headphone the song, "These Boots Are Made for Walkin!" I was ecstatic! I quickly told my mom about it, and we found the same song on her radio station, so she too could enjoy the visit from Daddy. This was the perfect affirmation that he heard my request and that he was with us. It really helped my mom to feel tremendously uplifted and joyful. She knew she wasn't going to be alone; Daddy could still hear us and would continue to be us.

"Thanks For The Memories," dear Daddy-O, and thank, You, most kind and loving, Father and Jesus, for allowing all of this. I am so very grateful.

CHRISTINE DUMINIAK

I Love You Always—Forever

My dear Papa Angel went Home to God a few years ago. He truly was an angel on earth, and I miss his smiling face and sense of humor tremendously. I suffer from an autoimmune disease, which causes a lot of physical pain and an inability to sleep well. I had been feeling very sad and depressed, so I really needed some encouragement from my Papa Angel.

One night when I was getting ready to feed my birds, I heard my dad's voice telling me to turn my radio on right away, so I did. Well, my heart did flip-flops when I heard the song "I Love You Always—Forever" playing, because that's what I always tell my Papa Angel when standing in front of his urn and praying for him. I guess he was telling me that he hears me and that he is never far away! I was so happy to hear that song, that I immediately started to cry. They were bittersweet tears because I wished with all my heart that I could have seen him! But I felt very loved that God had allowed me to hear my Papa Angel's voice in order to comfort me in my time of need.

LAURA HAYES

Teri....Teri

My grandmother and I were very close. She passed on October 10, 2001. I have had many after-death communications from her. One in particular that I remember was the very day my mamaw went Home to the Lord.

My brother Ashley came to drive my four daughters and me to my mother's house. My daughters were sitting in the back seat of the car. While en route to my mother's house, I thought I heard my girls call my name, "Teri," from the back seat of the car. I said to them, "Hold on a minute," as I was trying to regain my composure from my tears and pain from just losing my beloved mamaw. But I heard my name being called again, so I turned to answer them in the back seat and said, "What is it, girls?"

The children all looked at me as if I were crazy.

Looking for affirmation from my brother, I looked over at him and said, "Ashley, did you hear the girls call my name? And did you hear me answer them?" He just looked at me and said, "I thought you were talking to yourself!" Then I realized the voice had not called, "Mommy," as my kids normally would have. What I heard was a voice saying, "Teri .... Teri." I knew then it was my mamaw calling me, letting me know that she was still with me and that she lived on with the Lord.

TERI LYNN POWELL

Mom in the Ladies Room

My husband and I were out with some friends and I started talking to them about when my mom passed away. I explained to them that when I was by my mom's side in the hospital, she kept trying to mouth to me that she wanted to go home. She had a breathing tube, so it was hard for her to talk. I recognized that look in her eyes, as I had seen that same look when my dad was leaving earth. I knew that my mom was passing over soon, but she kept mouthing, "I want to go home."

Well this was very upsetting to me because every other time she had said this to me, I could and did take her back home. But I couldn't this time.

As we were sitting there with our friends talking, my husband told me that my mom really meant she wanted to go Home to God; that she wanted to see my dad. I started to cry, wondering if I had done the right thing by my mom. This had been bothering me for a long time and I had been praying to God about it. At that moment I excused myself from the table because I had to go to the ladies room.

While I was in the ladies room all alone, I heard a "shhhh" sound, as if someone was telling me to be quiet. I looked around and saw no one. Then I heard it again. It was my mom's voice and she said, "Shhhh. You don't have to keep wondering. Everything is fine. You don't have to keep talking about it."

Hearing my mom saying this to me made me feel so much better. I wished she were right in front of me so I could have seen her, for I would have loved to have hugged and kissed her right then and there. Wondering if I made the right decision for my mom had been eating at me since she passed, and now I knew she was all right. I have been waiting for an answer from mom about my decisions, and if I did the right thing, so I guess she had enough of my getting upset and always talking about it to my husband. Once again God came through and gave me a very special gift—my mother's voice and an answer to my prayers.

JUDIE ZIEGLER

Fire and Rain

My sister Lee and I were extremely close and I loved her dearly. We were both very spiritual people and shared this along with many other things.

After she passed away, we had her funeral service up North where we all grew up. Following her funeral, I drove down to Virginia Beach, where Lee had been living for a number of years. There was going to be a church memorial service for her there. My sister loved James Taylor's song, "Fire and Rain." Actually they were going to play this song at the church memorial service, but we didn't have enough room to record it on the tape, so, unfortunately, we had to leave it out. Lee must have been aware of this though, as you will see as you read on.

After the service I began my long trip back home and was just crossing over the Chesapeake Bay Bridge when I glanced over to look at the water. The sun was shining and glistening on the water and the view was breathtaking. I immediately thought of my sister and how much she loved Virginia Beach and living on the bay. She originally wanted to be cremated and have her ashes released in the bay, but changed her mind the last few days of her life.

As I watched the stunning sight of the sun glimmering on the water, I flipped around the stations of the radio, and the song, "Fire and Rain" by James Taylor was just coming on!

Now I have traveled this bridge many, many times over the years to visit my sister, and I had never been stopped on this bridge for any reason. There has never been a traffic tie-up at all! But now, while I was listening to "Fire and Rain" on the radio, the traffic never moved. It wasn't until the song was completely over that the traffic started up again. I was in total awe. I knew it was a gift from Lee. I could feel her presence.

A few weeks later, Lee continued to let me know she was there with me. It was the morning of our house move. The moving van was coming early that morning to move our things to our new house—a house that I wished with all my heart that Lee could have seen and shared in my joy. That morning, the radio alarm went off. As I lay there half-awake, I realized the song that woke me up on the radio was Lee's favorite song again, "Fire and Rain" by James Taylor! I was sooooo happy, for I knew that Lee was telling me she was with me for the move and would indeed share in my joy, which was my heart's desire.

I love you so much, Lee, and I know you are with me then, now, and forever. Love, Life And Laughter.

COLLEEN

Frank Sinatra

My dad Stanley loved music and loved to dance with my mom, his favorite jitterbug partner. Together they won many dance contests. When my dad was in the hospital near the end of his eighty-three years here on earth, in February 2000, I brought a tape recorder and played a Frank Sinatra tape all night long for him.

Even though my dad seemed out of it during my stay, I felt that he could subliminally enjoy one of his favorite singer's music which might be soothing to his mind, body, and soul.

While relaxing in Daddy's hospital room, I drifted off into a light sleep. During that state I was shown a sign from God that my dad would still be able to communicate with me, even after he transitioned over. I was shown a scene where my dad's hospital bed was empty. His pink bed sheets were very neatly turned down. Left behind on his empty bed was a rolled-up scroll with a string tied around it, indicating a message.

I woke up after having been shown this scene and intuitively knew that the scroll was a sign that there would be messages coming later on from my dad, after he had returned Home to God. This filled my heart with peace and the hope of a continuing, ongoing relationship with my dad.

A few days later my dad did cross over to God. True to the "scroll message" I had received, God has been blessing me tremendously by allowing many visits and messages from my dad. These visits have often been in the way of music and especially with Frank Sinatra music!

The Frank Sinatra music first started the same evening of my dad's passing. He came in the middle of the night and played a Frank Sinatra song in my head. It was one of the songs on the tape that I had played for him in the hospital.

Then every morning for the next nine months, while I was still groggy and lying in bed, I would be treated to hearing a song being played in my head! It would be either a Frank Sinatra song or another song that made a connection with my dad. I always knew this was a "Good Morning" from my dear dad, and it really made my day knowing that he would come by just to do this.

When that summer rolled around, Daddy's spirit followed me to an "Oldies Night" dance fest. The DJ was playing songs by Motown artists. Natalie, a friend of mine, and I were talking about ADCs and how exciting it was to get one. Natalie also knew about the many Frank Sinatra musical ADCs I had been getting from my dad since he passed.

A most unusual thing happened about ten minutes after talking about my Frank Sinatra ADCs from Dad. The DJ suddenly switched from Motown oldie to a single Frank Sinatra song, "Summer Wind!" After this, the DJ switched right back again to playing Motown oldie songs for the rest of the night!

Hearing a Frank Sinatra song being interjected this way, right smack in the middle of Motown music, was so bizarre! Natalie and I just looked at each other and burst out laughing. We knew the Frank Sinatra song was an obvious "Hello" from my dear dad, who surely heard us talking about him! My dad must have chosen "Summer Wind" because it is one of Natalie's favorite Frank Sinatra songs.

I realize that even though my dad is with God, he is still very much a part of my life. This is all thanks to God's kindness and compassion. God is showing us that love and relationships never die. They are as eternal as God and our immortal souls.

CHRISTINE DUMINIAK

Heaven, I'm In Heaven

My cousin Joanne lost her dad in October 1999. He was my Uncle Ray, my mom's brother. He passed ten months before my mom. I have had after-death communications from him on several occasions. Sometimes he even comes with my mom's spirit to visit me.

Joanne has been open to my discussing ADCs with her and has helped to fill in missing pieces of many of my ADCs concerning her dad. She has experienced some of her own afterlife signs and began asking me questions about ADCs.

One night, the most absolutely amazing thing happened and I'm still in awe of it. I got home rather late from my job, as a clinical social worker. I was putting dinner on the table a few minutes after 9 p.m. Now, I need to tell you that I do not know anything about Frank Sinatra at all, except his song "New York, New York." As I was setting the table, all of a sudden I began singing, "Heaven, I'm In Heaven." I had no idea that this was a Frank Sinatra song. Hey—I'm a child of the sixties! Give me the Monkees! Anyway, I stopped what I was doing and said to myself, "Where did that come from? I don't know that song." It wasn't as if I had been feeling great so I began to sing a happy tune. No! I had just had an awful session with one of my clients, and I came home feeling really defeated and frustrated.

After dinner I sat down at the computer and looked at my e-mail. The first e-mail was from my cousin Joanne. She said she took my advice and visited the Prayer Wave For After-Death Communication Message Board for the first time. She said what struck her first was reading about a Frank Sinatra music ADC the founder, Christine Duminiak, received from her dad. Uncle Ray, Joanne's dad, was a music buff. He lived for music. He loved all kinds of music, a favorite of his, though, was Frank Sinatra.

Anyway, Joanne's e-mail said that while on her way home from work, she stopped at a bookstore to get a book about after-death communications to learn more. Then she went next door to a Starbuck's café. As she sat there and began reading the book, a Frank Sinatra song came on. She said it was the song "Heaven, I'm In Heaven." She knew this was an ADC from her dad because today was the day she was so intrigued reading about someone's Frank Sinatra music ADC.

When I read this part of her e-mail, I think the color drained out of my face. I didn't even wait to e-mail her back. I ran for the phone. I needed to know what time she heard "Heaven, I'm In Heaven." It turned out, from the best we could figure, that I was singing the same song a few minutes after Joanne heard it!

I have never had an ADC like this before, but I really feel like my Uncle Ray was thanking me for helping Joanne to understand more about her after-death communications from him. Also, this would be a validation to Joanne that she couldn't ignore since we both experienced the same song at practically the same time. I feel certain that she will be having many ADCs from him now.

DIANE LOGIUDICE & JOANNE

* * *

* * *

CHAPTER 7

Birds, Animals & Insects

> Due to the supernatural powers of our loved ones' spirits, they are capable of visiting us in unique ways in order to be close to us. Usually this will be accompanied by some unusual behavior exhibited by an animal, bird, or insect along with the thought that this is a visit, no matter what they look like.

My Pet Dragonfly

I first became aware of dragonflies as being significant to the immediate passing of a loved one after my sister lost her baby Diana during her fifth month of pregnancy in July 1998. She had confided to me that she had suddenly spotted a lot of dragonflies in her backyard, and she wondered if it could have been the spirit of her daughter, Diana, who was named after Diana the Princess of Wales.

My own twenty-four-year-old son Jason crossed over to God thirteen months after his tiny cousin. Within two weeks of my son's journey back to God's paradise, I began encountering dragonflies in my backyard too. They would play above my head for hours!

One beautiful fall day in 2001, I went out to my car to drive to work. I had thoughts of my youngest sister on my mind that morning because she was due to have a baby any day. I was chosen to be the godmother, so I was anxiously awaiting the baby's birth. I then happened to notice the biggest, most beautiful dragonfly I had ever laid eyes upon sitting on the ground alongside my car. It was almost as if the dragonfly was patiently waiting for me to come out and to go on my way.

I leaned over and extended my finger towards the dragonfly, thinking it must be dying. It immediately clung to my finger. This creature showed absolutely no fear and I sensed my handling of it offered some immediate comfort.

With the dragonfly still clinging to my finger, I went into my house to get my digital camera because I knew I might have trouble getting anyone to believe my story of intimacy with this lovely dragonfly. At one point, the dragonfly flew off my finger and landed onto the lapel of my jacket. I instantly felt this loving dragonfly wanted to be closer to my heart!

The dragonfly spent about twenty minutes in my company, and I sensed all along it was my son's spirit wanting to spend time with me. I was so grateful for the miracle I was granted on that memorable, sunny day.

When the dragonfly and I were once again outside, the dragonfly unexpectedly flew off my finger and into the woods behind my house. I had an incredibly astounding and powerful thought come over me just then. I wondered if the dragonfly's visit was a sign from my son from beyond to fill my spirit with news of the impending birth of my godchild. In that one moment I felt as though I was in tune with the universe and was privy to a very big secret that no one else knew about—not even my pregnant sister.

I instinctively began to realize I may have received a very personal message from my son, reinforcing my belief that the relationship between a mother and child is never severed by death. Hours later, while at work, I got the exciting call that my sister suddenly went into labor in the early afternoon hours, just as she was about to go shopping. My newest niece and godchild Kassandra Marie was born safely and healthy! I felt like the luckiest woman in the world, not only because I had been blessed with a brand new niece to love, but also because I had been visited by a very special messenger from Heaven to let me know his new cousin was arriving that very day!

I was overjoyed at the wonder of it all because my son's spirit, arriving in the form of a dragonfly, was bridging the gap between Heaven and Earth, as my niece was making her transition from Heaven into our world. I will never stop believing in miracles bestowed upon us from the afterlife.

HELEN

Note from Christine Duminiak: Right after I read Helen's e-mail about this heartwarming dragonfly experience, I went outside to sit on our deck. It was then that I noticed a dragonfly! It was resting on our deck as if waiting for me. I felt this very timely appearance of a dragonfly was a validation from Jason's spirit to me that he had, indeed, visited his mother on that memorable day.

The Grasshopper

After my dad and my mother both passed, I found that I was receiving a lot of afterlife contacts through birds and even insects.

One day when I pulled up to my driveway I saw a bird sitting on top of my mailbox, as if it were waiting for me to come home. Then it flew off. I had the strong sensation that this bird was my mom and I said, "Awww, hi, Mom."

A few days later I had a dream about a grasshopper. Although I am not a fan of grasshoppers, in this dream I found myself placing a very sweet-looking grasshopper on my hand. At that moment in time in the dream, I just knew this was my dad's spirit and not really a grasshopper at all. I woke up right afterwards and smiled thinking about it. I felt that my dad had come to visit me.

The next day I called my sister and only told her about the bird on the mailbox. I never mentioned the dream about the grasshopper. Guess what she said to me? She said, "Today when I came home from work, there was a grasshopper sitting on my porch chair, just staring at me!" Hearing my sister talk about a grasshopper jogged my memory about the grasshopper dream I had the night before! So I told her that the grasshopper was dad, and I shared my dream with her. She was elated.

You see what I have learned in life is that our loved ones' spirits can briefly co-inhabit the bodies of birds, insects and animals, with their permission and God's.

CHRISTINE DUMINIAK

The Pigeon With A Sense of Humor

One day I was out in the yard, feeding the pigeons, and feeling sad and depressed. I was missing my dear dad, the light of my life, who now resides with God. Something happened that made me smile and laugh out loud because I knew that it was my Papa angel that caused this to happen.

While I was bending over to put food in the birds' food dish, one of the pigeons decided to contentedly land on my rear end! I thought that this was so hilarious and it really made my whole afternoon.

I just could not help smiling after that because that was very definitely my Papa Angel's great sense of humor, and he would have loved seeing that. Wait a minute, what am I saying? He did see that, and in fact, he arranged for that to happen! Well, I do hope that I was able to make you smile, or even hopefully laugh!

LAURA HAYES

Daddy Was The Deer

In the summer of 2000, a few months after my dad was called Home, my mother, sisters, husband and I were at our mountain house. It was a mini-vacation meant to comfort all of us. We greatly missed dad.

One afternoon while there, my mother and sister were relaxing out on the back deck overlooking the lake and the woods. Along came a friendly, docile deer. It stopped, turned his head, and just stared at them. He acted as if he knew them. Then this deer proceeded to take its front leg and stamp the ground with his hoof three times trying to get their attention. His hoof actions were similar to what horses do. Then the deer continued to stare at them while grazing the foliage. He was not afraid of them at all. He seemed to relaxed and comfortable as if he belonged to them.

My sister thought this was the most amazing sight. She excitedly ran into the house to summon me to come out and observe this unusual deer. So I grabbed my dog Sandy into my arms, and I joined them on the deck. Sandy started to bark at the deer. Normally deer are very skittish around people and noises, but this deer refused to be scared off by the barking. It just kept grazing and staring at us. It even repeated its hoof stamping three times on the ground for me.

After a long while the deer eventually strolled off leaving us gaping in amazement.

I didn't get the connection to my dad's spirit until a little later when my mom suddenly blurted out, "If your dad were here, he would have said, 'Oh don't be afraid of that deer.'" BINGO. I had that aha moment. *That deer was my dad!* I knew that our loved ones' spirits have the supernatural God-given ability to briefly co-inhabit the bodies of animals, birds and insects, but I wanted to be sure if this was my dad.

So that night as I lay in bed and prayed, I asked out loud, "Dad, were you that deer today?" To my surprise and delight, I was shown a vision of a horse counting with its hoof! This was my answer! Yes, indeed this was our dad who was vacationing with us up the mountains. How kind of God to have sent him to us in this precious way.

CHRISTINE DUMINIAK

Ten Birds From Ashley

I was outside one morning sitting on my porch thinking of my twenty-three-year-old dear brother Ashley, who went Home to God three months earlier. While sitting there, I noticed there were a lot of birds in my yard. I decided to get some bird food and hoped that, if I threw some nearby, they would come closer; instead they got scared and flew away. I waited awhile longer to see if they would return, and when they didn't I decided to run some errands.

As I drove out of my driveway, a single bird flew right in front of my car. I thought to myself how odd that was. The bird came so close to my car that I thought I might actually hit it. On my way to and from the store this happened repeatedly. A single bird would fly from one side of the road to the other, right in front of my car. I counted a total of ten birds, with the tenth bird crossing in front of my car as I pulled into my driveway. I thought about the number ten and what was its significance. Then I remembered that my little brother Ashley was born on the 10th of September!

A little while later my neighbor called to tell me that there were *ten* red birds hanging around her pool deck and what a beautiful sight it was. Since I had not talked to her at all that day, she hadn't known about the ten birds I saw flying in front of my car earlier and the significance it had to me. So I shared my story with her and laughed when I realized it was my brother Ashley's way of saying, "Hello, Sis."

On this very day my mother had been out buying a CD with a few songs on it about the love of a mother and her child. One of the songs talked about the birth of a son. You see my mother, who lost her twenty-three-year-old son Ashley, was remembering him and the day he was born. She was remembering giving birth to him on the 10th of September. I believe my brother knew this, and he was letting us know that he knew that she was thinking of him, loving him, and missing him. He was saying "Hello, Mom, I love you too."

TERI LYNN POWELL (ASHLEY'S BIG SISTER)

The Hawk Who Golfs With Me

Since my dear dad was called back home to God, I've received many hawk ADCs from him, especially while golfing. You see, my dad used to be my favorite golf buddy.

He first established his distinctive "hawk" method of communicating with me about eight months after he passed over. My husband and I were standing on top of a mountain in the Poconos on a beautiful, bright autumn day, and I happened to notice there were two hawks circling overhead. I started to sense that this was a sign from my dad. I believe his spirit had given me that thought, and I started to smile thinking it was the spirit of my dad flying high above us in the sky, and how much fun he was having in being be able to do this.

A little later we were on our way back home. My husband had been driving for about an hour, and I dozed off and had a dream. The dream was about two hawks flying in the sky right above our car as we were traveling along the highway. Abruptly, I awoke from this hawk dream and glanced upwards at the front windshield and saw, to my great amazement, there were in fact two hawks flying overhead—exactly like in my dream! This was a clear sign to me that my dad was using hawks to visit me.

After this, I started to notice that a lone hawk would show up whenever I was out golfing. It didn't matter where I was—at home in the city or up the mountains—a hawk would appear, circle above me, and then fly off. I knew it was a hello from my dad's spirit flying over me because we loved to golf together. I treasured his "hawk" visits. It really touched me and was a balm to my aching heart.

On one occasion in particular, while golfing I had an amazing supernatural encounter with my dad's spirit: My husband and I were asked to play golf with two men we didn't know. I felt a bit intimidated because I didn't want to embarrass myself by playing poorly, which I was more than capable of doing! So before each golf shot, I said a prayer asking for God's help. I was also talking to my dad, asking for his help too, and then some wonderful ADCs started to happen.

First, I saw a lone hawk circle overhead, which was my dad's sign that he was "golfing" with me. I knew I was going to be getting some major help now, so I smiled, said hello to my dad, and began to relax. Then a little later that day, something unbelievably phenomenal happened on the golf course! I had been discussing with my hubby a really good golf tip my dad had given me. I said, "My dad used to constantly tell me to 'hit down on the ball,' and this golf tip greatly helped me to hit a solid golf shot because my hips would naturally move down correctly during my swing."

After having said this, about five minutes went by. I was in the middle of my swing when I suddenly felt *a powerful force grab ahold of my hips and actually pull my hips down just as I was hitting the ball!* And boy did my shot really go far! I knew I had just gotten some "hands on" help from my dear dad! And I couldn't get over that he could do that! (Nice one, Dad!)

Because of the innumerable times I received heavenly help that day, I ended up having the best round of golf in my entire life, with my lowest score ever—an 89! It was a great day full of demonstrative ADCs, blessings, fun, and love.

I know God has been blessing me with these loving and wonderful after-death communications from my dear dad, and I am so very thankful. These contacts always make me smile and feel very loved and cared for. Thank You, dear Jesus, for your kindness and thank you, dear Daddy-O. I love you both!

CHRISTINE DUMINIAK

Hundreds and Hundreds of Dragonflies

I remember when I was a little girl on a fishing boat with my brother, and if a dragonfly would come around the boat, my brother would scare me by saying, "Watch out, Cathy Ann, it will sew your ears up." Little did I know that later in life a dragonfly would mean communication from our precious son John, who crossed over to God on August 24, 2000, at age 25.

AFTER-DEATH COMMUNICATIONS

The first time that dragonflies appeared was at my son's funeral service held at the gravesite. At the time, I did not notice them but a woman at work said, "I have been meaning to ask you, did you see the hundreds of dragonflies surrounding the service? There were hundreds." And I sadly said, "No, I didn't see them."

The second time dragonflies made their appearance was at the first anniversary of my son's passing. My husband and I, with my son's best friend and his family, all went to the park where John's memorial bench is located at a point on the lake. We were planning on releasing balloons in John's memory. When we got to the memorial bench, the dragonflies around us were in the hundreds! There were so many there that there was not a spot where you could not see them. Well, we all tied our blue balloons together and held each other and let them go and watched them until they were out of sight. When we looked behind us, after watching the balloons float skyward, the dragonflies were gone.

The third time we saw dragonflies involved my husband, who had to make a truck delivery to the heart institute where we last held and saw our son. This was painful for my husband, but since it was his job, he felt he had to make the delivery anyway. So he backed up the truck to the loading dock at the hospital. A man on the dock said, "Come here, you have got to see this!" The whole outside area of the loading dock near his truck was covered with dragonflies, hundreds of them!

The fourth time I saw a dragonfly was while I was walking into work one morning. I saw one single dragonfly sitting on the sidewalk. Even though I stood very close to it and watched it, the dragonfly never felt fear; it did not fly away even though my presence was so close to it. This event may not seem unusual, until you tie it in with a later dragonfly's appearance at my place of work, which I will explain a little later.

The fifth time was the day after we had seen the movie Dragonfly. My husband was outside working on our property and called me at home from his cell phone. He said, "Cathy, I am surrounded by dragonflies!" He was just so happy and I said, "Hon, it is your son; he loves you so much."

The sixth time I saw dragonflies was after I had been feeling sorry for myself on a Saturday, and I stayed in bed most of the day. When Sunday came and I started to feel the same way, I said to myself, "Get dressed, go out into the Memorial Garden you have for your son John, and make it look like you care!" The Memorial Garden was overgrown with weeds. So I forced myself to get dressed, clean up the weeds, and tidy up the garden. Feeling exhausted, I collapsed in a swing in the garden to watch the pink sunset, and then it happened! Hundreds of dragonflies came flying right over the swing where I was sitting! They stayed for about ten minutes. As I looked at the sunset and watched the amazing number of dragonflies, I said to my son, "Babe, you liked that Mom got out and did this for you, didn't you?" I know my John was smiling at me in approval and appreciated the strength it took for me to pull myself together to do this out of my love for him.

The seventh time a dragonfly came into our lives turned out to be a really phenomenal ADC. I had gotten a call from my husband, and I could tell, just by his excitement, that he had received another sign from our son. Here is what happened. My husband was at work, driving in his semi and talking to our son in spirit, as he does day after day. This particular day he was telling John that his work gloves were so worn, that they were no longer protecting his hands. He told John that he needed to stop at a store really soon to buy some new ones.

Well, he continued to drive down the road, and up ahead, on the side of the road, was something just lying there. My husband felt a strong desire to investigate further, so he pulled off the road and got out of the semi. As he got closer, he noticed that lying on the side of the road was a brand new, heavy-duty pair of work gloves. Not only that, but sitting on top of the gloves was a DRAGONFLY—a dragonfly being a sign from our son!

John had seen to it that his dad's hands were protected and the dragonfly came to say, "Dad, I love you."

The eighth time a dragonfly came into my life, in a most unusual fashion, was when I was walking and talking to a co-worker on our way to work. We were headed towards the main doors of the office building, when a lone dragonfly began circling my legs. My co-worker was just inside the door, but I couldn't go in because of the dragonfly surrounding me. The dragonfly then decided to land right by my foot. I bent down and put my finger by his legs and he got on my finger and clenched it tightly! I lifted him up and looked at him; he was so cute. I decided that I needed to place him in a safe environment, so I walked to a bush by the building and placed him gently on that bush and continued on my way to work thinking about this unusual experience.

Was this John's spirit visiting me? I think so.

While not knowing the entire meaning of the dragonfly, John's dad and I believe the meaning to us is this: Our son's spirit wants to surround us with one of God's small creatures, the dragonfly, or at times even briefly be a dragonfly himself. Dragonflies, while their lives are short, accomplish their plan on this earth—like our son did. His time here on earth was short, but he achieved his dream of a college education even though he was ill all of his life. We are so proud of you, John!

CATHYJMF & JOHN MURTAUGH

CHAPTER 8

Children's Experiences

Children seem to have a gift of being able to see and hear spirits. When they are talking to an imaginary friend, please take them seriously, for they may be talking to Jesus, angels or loved ones.

Shopping with Angel Sissy

Since I lost my husband to a work-related accident a number of years ago, I have been praying to God to get ADCs for myself and for my friends. And as a result of my search about the afterlife, I have been blessed to become best friends with another woman in grief, who lost her beloved daughter named Sissy. We met through the Internet and are both part of the Prayer Wave For After-Death Communication Group. She feels like my other half, for we have shared so much and we are that close.

My story is this: My sister and her family were down for the weekend to spend Christmas with us. I had spent the day with my four-year-old nephew Thomas. He and I went into the city, did some shopping, and went out to McDonald's for lunch.

Thomas is a very "in touch" little four-year-old. He talks to his Uncle Tommy (my husband who passed) all the time. Well, as we were walking around the grocery store in the city, he was chattering away to me about this and that, all those things little four-year-old boys talk about when, suddenly, he went very silent. I asked him, "Thomas, what's the matter?"

He looked at me and said, "Aunt Marie, Who's Sissy?" I was in shock when I heard the name Sissy and with my heart racing I said, "What did you just say, Thomas?" He repeated, "Who's Sissy?" I said, "Well that's my friend's daughter. Why do you ask?" He said, "No, Aunt Marie, Sissy is an angel!" I said, "Yes, Thomas, you're right. Sissy is an angel, just like Uncle Tommy is." He looked at me with this great big smile on his face and said, "Aunt Marie, this angel is shopping with us!"

I'm sure I looked like a crazy woman in the store, as I spun around and asked, "Where is she, Thomas?" He laughed and said, "She's riding in the cart with me, Aunt Marie. She thinks this is fun!" So I laughed and said, "No wonder the cart is so heavy– pushing the two of you around with all these groceries, and she better not be sitting on the bread!" He giggled and said, "Aunt Marie, she's an angel. She isn't going to squish the bread."

So I kept this conversation going all through the grocery store asking him repeatedly, "Is Sissy still here?" He would smile and say, "Yes, she's blowing on my cheek giving me butterfly kisses." I asked him, "What is she saying?" And he said, "She says, 'I love her,'" and Thomas pointed to me. Then he said, "She said to say, everything will be okay!"

So we went to pay for the groceries and Thomas was chattering away, giggling, smiling and nodding his head yes, etc., etc. The lady at the cash register said to me, "Looks like someone has an imaginary friend." I just smiled, but Thomas looked at her and said, "No, lady, I have an angel; her name is Sissy!"

The cashier gave me this "yeah, right" look. I said to her, "He's not lying, he has an angel with him." Well, the cashier looked at me, as though she was getting ready to call in the psych doctors to have me committed!

After Thomas and I got into the car, I asked Thomas if Sissy was coming with us for a ride? He said, "Nope, Aunt Marie, she had to go. Someone else needed her right now, but she will be back!" This was truly an awesome experience!

MARIE

A Heavenly Hug

My wife Cathy passed in August 2000. After reading many spiritual books and having enlightening and validating sessions with the medium, Sunni Welles, I had come to know how to ask and receive the name of my main guardian angel. So while talking to my seven-year-old granddaughter Ashley about Grandma Cathy's passing, I asked Ashley to find out her own angel's name. Before going to sleep and rebuking Satan, little Ashley asked Our Lord to know her angel's name. Upon waking, the name "Theresa" was given to Ashley.

On Christmas Day, Ashley and I were standing in the garage at her other grandparents' house. I asked her if she had talked to her Angel Theresa lately. Ashley was busy playing with some new toys and paused for a moment, then turned to me and said, "Yes, Theresa loves me very much." I then asked Ashley, "Have you been able to talk to Grandma Cathy?" She stood up and walked over to me and put her little arms around me and said, "This is for you from Grandma. She misses us all, but she misses you the most Grandpa. Grandma hears all that you say and is with us every day." We both stood still as a wonderful chill filled both of us and then faded away. Ashley's eyes were wide open and asked, "What *was* that?" I explained that Grandma Cathy had just given both of us a heavenly hug. Ashley went back to her toys, and I felt terrific after getting the best Christmas present I could have received.

PAT D.

Daddy and the Bright Light

My brother left behind three sons—Mark, Todd, and Sean—when he died suddenly at the young age of thirty-five. His youngest son Sean, who was only about six years old, was with him when he collapsed on the floor of their kitchen. He had been getting Sean a glass of milk when he suffered a cerebral hemorrhage and never regained consciousness. Sean was greatly affected by this because of the way his father died right in front of him. It left him feeling very lost and not really believing that his father was gone.

About two weeks after my brother's death, Sean had climbed into bed with his mother because he was still afraid to sleep by himself. The bathroom was just a couple of doors away from the bedroom. Sean noticed that there was a light coming from the door, which was very bright, not like a regular bathroom light. He heard his name being called. The voice said, "Sean, come to me. It's Dad." Well Sean was very scared, but he recognized his dad's voice. The voice called to him again saying, "Don't be afraid. It's Dad."

Sean got out of bed and went towards the light. The bathroom door slowly opened, and Sean saw his father bathed in a brilliant white light. He told him not to be afraid, that he would always be with him, and then he was gone. Sean is now thirty-five years old and still remembers this. He feels that this appearance by his dad helped him get through his father's death. Sean believes very much in after-death communication and we have talked about this many times.

MONIQUE MOORE

Uncle Brian's Spirit Watched The Ceremony

When our youngest son Brian was murdered in June of 1989, my first grandson (Ryan) was only eighteen months old. Brian loved Ryan so much and he was so proud to be an uncle for the first time. Ryan doesn't remember his Uncle Brian; he only knows him through pictures and stories.

My daughter Lisa (Ryan's mother) and I have experienced numerous ADCs after Brian's death, but I never expected my grandson to experience them, much less talk about them. I really don't know when Ryan started to experience ADCs, but he started telling me about them when he was around 12 years old. Here are some of the spiritual sightings and contacts that Ryan experienced.

We attended Ryan's "Moving On Ceremony" at his middle school. The next day Ryan told me that, while he was marching into the auditorium, he could sense Brian was with him. Ryan knew that he was there watching the ceremony. He also told me that he could sense "a lot of dead spirits" there in the auditorium. This is Ryan's terminology. Ryan said that he couldn't actually see them in human form, but saw their colors and could sense their spirits.

I told Ryan I was sure that, with all the people there, a lot of them had lost loved ones, and that those loved ones were also there enjoying the ceremony.

He also told me that, at times, he can feel someone's hand on his shoulder. If he is in school, he will turn his head to see who it is, yet no one is there. Ryan told me that he knows that it's Brian though. It makes me feel good to know that Brian is watching over his nephew.

Another day Ryan had a half-day of school and was at my house. I was in the living room reading, and Ryan came down the stairs into the living room. All of a sudden he stopped and said, "B." (That's what my grandchildren call me—"B.") I said, "What, Honey?"

Ryan said, "B, Brian is standing over in the corner."

"What does he look like?" I asked.

He said that he didn't see a form standing there but a colored cloud. I asked what color the cloud was and he said a bluish color. I looked and didn't see anything, but I believed him, as I cannot explain all the many spiritual happenings that we have experienced since Brian's death.

Ryan and I walked into the kitchen to get something and we both heard a loud thump that came from the living room. I assumed that something had fallen, so we both went into the living room to find out what it was. I looked over at the corner of the room where Ryan, just a few minutes earlier, said he had seen Brian. I have a three-tiered shelf on the wall in that area of the living room. Standing on the shelf are tiny Dreamsicle Angels; however, two of the angels were now lying on their sides. It would have been impossible for them to have fallen over by themselves because they are so tiny. The noise we heard was loud enough for Ryan and me to hear clear into the next room. We were meant to hear it, so we would come out and investigate.

I told Ryan that it was a validation that he did, indeed, see Brian in the corner of the room. It also validated for me that the white glowing light, I sometimes see at night over the door to the entrance of what was Brian's bedroom, is Brian's spirit watching over us. Having experienced so many ADCs in my lifetime from Brian, and a few from my grandfather, I know that it is truly a gift from God.

PHYLLIS HOTCHKISS AND RYAN LUSBY

AFTER-DEATH COMMUNICATIONS

The Toy Telephone

My sister Joni had a problem with her uterus, which kept her from carrying her babies to full term. She lost three babies who were born prematurely. She loved children and would have been a wonderful mother, but it was not meant to be.

When I started having children we asked Joni and her husband to be godparents to ours. Who better to be godmother to my children than my sister?

In April 1999, I found out I was once again pregnant. What a surprise to my entire family, including my husband and me! Joni was very excited; she could not wait to find out if it was a girl or a boy, but to her it made no difference. She just loved children.

On July 19, 1999, Joni suffered a seizure at her job. We found out a week later that she had a tumor in her brain, and it was cancerous. The doctor said he could prolong her life for a little while but she had a year, perhaps two years, to live. All I could think about was that Joni was not going to see my baby grow up and my baby not remembering her. I wanted desperately for the baby to remember her. I prayed and prayed and prayed for Joni.

My two older children, Matt (thirteen) and Lindsey (eleven), were very close with Joni. She often took them to her house to sleep over, to the movies, and would talk to them on the phone. In fact, when my older children were babies, Joni would always tell me, "Put him on the phone. Let him talk to me. Let me talk to her." She always talked to them on the phone. This was her thing. My sister and I also talked a lot on the phone.

One night when we were talking on the phone together, Joni had a lot of questions about the afterlife. She couldn't understand why her babies or our grandmothers never tried to contact us and let us know they were all right. I told her I didn't know why, but I guessed that there was a reason why they didn't. Maybe because they were happy or just didn't feel they needed to. I didn't have an answer for her.

During the course of her cancer and my last pregnancy, we spent a lot of time together. She came to doctor visits with us. She even came to the ultrasound procedure with us to find out the sex, where we found out that we (my husband, sister and I) were having a baby boy.

In October 1999, we had our baby boy Jared Michael. I wanted that name because I liked it and Joni liked it too. He was the apple of her eye—her reason for living. We spent as much time with Joni as possible, making sure she and Jared had plenty of quality time together. She would do things like grease his hair up into a little curl and buy him toys—one being a toy telephone. The day she brought that toy phone over, she said emphatically, "He has to have a phone!" I didn't think a whole lot of it at the time—not until later.

As time went on Joni started to deteriorate. Her brain swelling wasn't going down after her second surgery. The doctors really couldn't do much more for her. She was able to celebrate Jared's first birthday with us, but didn't quite make it to his second birthday. She passed over on September 9, 2001.

Nine days after Joni's passing I was upstairs alone in the bathtub. I was thinking about my sister and was remembering our conversation about the afterlife. I simply said aloud, "Joni, did you get your answers?" I went downstairs and called my mother-in-law to wish her a happy birthday. After we hung up I relaxed on the sofa. My older children, Matt and Lindsey, were also in the living room.

Jared, who was close to two-years-old, was going about his own business playing with his cars as he always did. After a while I noticed him digging through his toys in the toy box and throwing them out in different directions. I figured he was looking for cars; that was all he played with anymore. The next thing I knew, I heard him saying, "Joey! Joey! Hi, Joey!" (He called Joni–Joey.) Jared was not only talking to Joey, but sending her kisses on that toy telephone as well!

I remember sitting straight up and looking at him and watching him on that toy telephone.

I asked Matt and Lindsey when they last remembered seeing him play with that phone. They said, what I had thought, that it had been a very long time since he played with that phone. We knew that my sister Joni was communicating with Jared on that toy phone, just like she always used to do. I realized then that Joni had, indeed, gotten her answers about the afterlife and was trying to let me know this through my son Jared.

JENNI

* * *

AFTER-DEATH COMMUNICATIONS

* * *

CHAPTER 9

Coins

> The coin you find may have a significant date to you, or you may find that one materializes mysteriously when you are in need of comfort. You may even notice a pattern being repeated.

Pennies from Heaven

My sister Lori passed over on a Saturday. My first penny ADC came on a Saturday. I was sitting in the Wal-Mart parking lot thinking of her and asking her to come and visit me. When I got out of my truck to head for the store, I looked down and found two pennies by my truck.

My second penny ADC came the following Saturday. I was to go motorcycle riding with my hubby. Before leaving, I was looking for something that belonged to my sister so I could take it with me. I felt the added protection would be good, but I couldn't find anything. When we got home, I was changing clothes and a penny fell out of my pocket. I didn't know where it came from, though, for I had no change on me when I left.

My third penny ADC came a few weeks later, again on a Saturday. My mom had received worrisome news that her blood platelet count was up. I was sitting in my truck getting ready to leave for the store. I bowed my head and prayed and begged for Lori to visit our mom. When I opened my eyes there was a penny sitting on my lap! There is no other way that this penny could have landed on my lap except that it came from Heaven.

Although I wanted to believe the other incidences of "Saturday pennies" were a sign from my sister Lori, I really didn't believe they were, until this last incident when one just materialized on my lap, after my prayer.

DEBBIE

Eric "Dropped" By With a Penny

Our son Eric returned Home to God in December 1997. Since then, we have gotten many ADCs from him, which never ceases to amaze us.

We have been finding pennies from Eric for years now and believe it is when and where you find them that is important and meaningful.

On one occasion when we visited our house, which was under construction, I left a footprint in the mud near the outside entrance. No one was around and I had no change in my pocket, and my wife Marilyn left her purse in the car. When we came out thirty minutes later on top of my footprint was a brand new penny. A sign from above.

Marilyn and I have noticed that sometimes the penny that will be left will be the year that you lost a loved one. We always check the date but had no luck until recently.

I play golf with the Grasscutters, a group for new people to the area, who play different golf courses at a really reasonable fee. We were playing a golf course called Foxfire. Because there is water across the second hole, you have to be able to hit your tee shot about two hundred and sixty yards in order to make it safely over the water. I made mention to my foursome that my son Eric's and my tee shots both carried over the water when we played there seven years ago. My group agreed that these were great drives, and I was happy to able to do it again that day. As we drove up to my tee shot, I was thinking about where Eric's ball and my ball landed that day seven years ago. We stopped the cart so I could address my ball for my second shot. Right beside my ball was a penny dated 1997–the same year as Eric's passing!

Then on another occasion, we were together with a friend of ours named Nick. Nick was close to our son Eric, and he watched our house while we took care of funeral arrangements. After some time passed, Nick and I were going to be golfing together. The night before Nick and I went golfing, we talked for hours about the afterlife and signs, etc.

The next day when Nick and I and two others were golfing together, Nick brought up the subject of the penny I found at Foxfire's Golf Club. After this penny ADC conversation we found ourselves on the tenth hole. Three of us teed up our balls, except for Nick. We all were at the same spot to hit our drives. But when it was Nick's turn, and he placed his tee in the ground in that very same spot where we all just hit from, and he started to cry. He found a penny there, yet, it wasn't there a minute ago!

Nick had to sit in the golf cart for a few minutes to reflect on this and to regain his composure, as he had never had anything like that happen to him before. I believe that he got the penny as a thanks for his help, as well as an affirmation.

We believe that the pennies are for reinforcement and acknowledgment; that our loved ones are still with us and choose to help us at special times—not always in times of grief and not all the time.

It was amazing to be a part of something so miraculous and so mysterious; yet, I understand so clearly what and why this is happening—to reinforce our knowledge of the afterlife and to continue to help others who have had losses.

FRED & MARILYN ZIMMERMAN

Now You See It, Now You Don't

My dear son Braden died in an accident in March 2001. We have gotten some wonderful ADCs from him, and I would like to share with you one that I received around January 2003.

I was feeling really overwhelmed with work at the beginning of the school year. The term had just started, and I was teaching overtime and teaching a class that had me prepping for hours, when I should have been doing administrative work instead. After the second school week, I had "had it." In what was very unusual behavior for me, I got home from work, sat down on the couch, and proceeded to bawl my head off in front of my husband. I told him that I didn't know how I could possibly manage the stress, that I had never felt this way before, and that I was anxious and very upset.

He immediately began to comfort me. As I sat there crying, he held me and said a prayer asking God to take care of me during these hard times. Then he had to leave for an appointment. I sat there by myself crying for a while when some force, beyond my control, made me get up, go into the spare bedroom, and start rooting around in my jewelry box.

Well, first of all I don't wear jewelry, so I rarely look in the jewelry box, and that explains why it's in the spare bedroom. I had in my mind that I was, for whatever reason, looking for a pair of earrings a friend had left behind one day. The box was high up on a hutch, so I couldn't see what I was feeling. Still crying, I opened the first bottom drawer on the right and rummaged around blindly. Suddenly I felt a coin. I thought, "Oh well, parking money." I pulled it out and got one of the biggest shocks of my life. As the tears were still spilling down my cheeks, I found myself staring at a quarter with a small note on white paper taped to it. I was dumb struck. It read in Braden's handwriting, "For good luck on the job!" and when I turned it over, he had put his initials (B.L.) three times on the back. He must have given this quarter to me years ago and I had forgotten all about it.

When my husband came home and I told him about this, he was shocked. We both thanked Braden and God for the incredibly timely message. I felt much better after that, of course, knowing I was being taken care of.

Now for the second part of this wonderful ADC. My husband wanted to somehow frame the special quarter from Braden or put it in a case, so that I could have it nicely preserved. I had the quarter on top of the entertainment center in the living room, so I could look at it whenever I wanted to gain some much needed strength, due to my exhaustive schedule. I had the quarter for about two weeks, when about that time my husband put the coin in a "safe" place to frame it for my birthday present. He then promptly forgot where he had put it!

Well, we looked everywhere and I was devastated. During that time of searching, the wall-to-wall rug in the living room was removed and a laminate floor was laid down. A few weeks after losing my special quarter, I was again feeling down about work and had mentioned it to my husband by cell phone, as he was on his way home from work. His response was that I had never acted like this before about work, so things must be really rough, and he'd keep on praying for me.

I hung up the phone, looked down at the floor by my feet, and there right in front of me was the missing quarter!

My husband says it must be the work of God and Braden. There was no way, after pulling up the rug and replacing it with flooring, that it would suddenly appear there, especially since my husband had purposely taken it, and every other valuable thing, out of the living room before putting down the new floor.

VICKI TALBOTT

* * *

CHAPTER 10

Comas

> Spirits seem to be very alive, aware, and even travel when they are in a coma-like state. If you feel that you didn't get a chance to say goodbye because your loved one was in a coma, please don't worry, for they heard you then and continue to hear you after they transition over to God. This is, without a doubt, a huge blessing from God.

Jimmy and Aunt Donnis' Comas

A few years ago my brother Jimmy was burned really badly in a fire while he was burning brush that was at the bottom of his land. There was a gas can nearby and it exploded and burned him terribly. He was taken by ambulance to a trauma burn unit in North Carolina where, after three days, he went into a coma. We stayed by his side night and day.

Meanwhile, at the same time, my Aunt Donnis was in Carolina's Medical Center in the critical care unit with scleroderma, and she also was in a coma. Our family took turns as to who stayed with whom and we traveled back and forth for months, so that neither my aunt nor my brother would be alone. Eventually, we were told that Aunt Donnis was dying and nothing further could be done for her—it was just a matter of time. We were all very sad about this, and with Jimmy's being so badly off at the same time, it was doubly difficult.

The day Jimmy woke up from his coma, he asked, "How's Don?" (Aunt Donnis). We didn't want to upset him, so we didn't tell him the whole truth—that she was dying. We just told him she was still very ill. But Jimmy said, "That can't be right; she was just here yesterday." We told him she wasn't, but Jimmy insisted that she was and he said, "Yes she was; she was right here. She told me I had to wake up; that all this was too much on Momma; that I had to fight because Momma was really gonna need me. So I told Don I would, and she said, 'I love you, Jimmy, see ya later.'" Well, we were just amazed at this visit, for we knew there was no way this could've happened because Aunt Donnis was in a coma in a different location at the time. Two weeks later, Aunt Donnis passed over.

It was now the day of the viewing for Aunt Donnis, and we decided we had to tell Jimmy about her death. Even though he was now home, he wouldn't be able to attend the funeral. We went to Jimmy's house and told him that Aunt Donnis had passed. Jimmy was devastated, but he now understand this was why she had come to him while they were both in comas. Jimmy said, "Bring Momma to me when the funeral is over; she needs me." So we did. Two years later, Jimmy passed too. Maybe that's what Aunt Donnis meant when she said to Jimmy, "See ya later."

CANDI HOLLIFIELD

Golfing To Country Roads

One day in 2009 I was golfing with my husband when I received a sad call on my cell phone from my sister. She wanted to let me know that her good friend's husband (Joe) just passed over after a long bout with brain cancer.

I stopped for a few minutes and said a prayer for all of them. As I approached the next tee box and got ready to hit my tee shot, I started to spontaneously and uncontrollably sing out loud the song, "Country Roads" by John Denver.

I stopped and said to my husband, "I can't believe this, but I am singing "Country Roads," and I don't know why. It was like something came over me that forced me to sing this particular song."

So I called my sister and asked her to find out if the song "Country Roads" had any significance to her friend whose husband Joe just passed.

The next day my sister called me to tell me the shocking evidentiary news! Whenever Joe would get into his car with his son, the first song that he would play on his CD player was–you guessed it–"Country Roads!" I know this was a validation of Joe's hearing my prayers for him and his family and to get a message to them, that he was with them.

CHRISTINE DUMINIAK

Steve's Country Roads

We received a phone call on June 5, 2002, telling us that my brother Steve, who I hadn't seen in eighteen months, was in a coma. I come from a family of ten children and am the third from the youngest. I've always been the one who stood back and let everyone else do for the family.

I abhorred hospitals and did not like being around sick people. However, when the phone call came about my brother Steve being in a coma, I told my boss I had to go. Something in my heart said nothing else mattered, and it didn't. We left that day to drive the eleven hours it would take us to get there.

When we finally arrived, the hospital staff told us he wasn't doing well; he had cirrhosis, hepatitis C, and other infections. Steve was in a coma that he would never come out of. When I saw my brother all I wanted to do was hold his hand. The whole time I was there, I gently held onto Steve's hand as I made my amends to him. I constantly told him that I loved him and I was sorry for not being the sister I should have been.

Two days later, the hospital staff told us that he had minimal brain activity, and we needed to think about taking him off of the ventilator. After a few days, we agreed to have Steve taken off of the ventilator. One of the nurses said she didn't know how long it would be before he would pass over. But my brother surprised all of us. While still in a coma, he started breathing on his own. It was very labored breathing though. Around midnight the nurse told us it might be hours or days before he actually did pass. Upon hearing the inevitable prognosis, one of my sisters in the room started singing my brother's favorite song in order to comfort him, which was "Country Roads."

The nurse told me that there were two things she could do for him. She said she could either give him a bath or give him some morphine to make him more comfortable. I asked her to give him a bath. We stepped outside of his room to give him some privacy. When we re-entered his room a little later, the curtain was still drawn, so we went downstairs not thinking "death," but a bath.

While we were downstairs, we felt this cool breeze come out of nowhere and made a mental note about it. After a little while, we went back upstairs to Steve's room. When we arrived, the nurse informed us that my brother had passed not even five minutes after we left his room. As we were getting ready to leave Steve's hospital room for the last time, the TV was still on and Steve's favorite song "Country Roads" started to play! We were amazed at the timing of this and felt it was a sign from Steve. It also helped us to realize that he heard my sister sing his favorite song to him, even though he was in a coma! His spirit had heard it.

Four months later on October 11, 2002, Christine Duminiak had contacted me to check to see if the edited version of my "Country Roads" ADC story from my brother for this book was accurate. Later on that same night, I was thinking about Steve as I was lying in bed and channel surfing the TV. I really couldn't find anything that held my interest; however, I did come across a commercial that was playing 70s music. They were selling twenty CDs or twenty cassettes. While watching the commercial, I started having feelings of dèjá vu. Then it hit me! This was the same TV commercial that was playing the song "Country Roads" the night my brother passed in the hospital!

At first I said, "Wow, an ADC from Steve," and then the skeptic in me said, "No, this can't be." But I looked over at the clock in my room and the time showed 2:47 a.m. Now none of the clocks in my home are set to the correct time, and I don't know how long this commercial had already been on before I found it, but I know we were told that my brother Steve passed at 2:41 a.m., which was pretty darn close to the time on my clock!

I believe that Steve was guiding me to channel surf so that I would come across that same TV commercial with "Country Roads" again, for he knew I was thinking about him. It was his gift to me to let me know he was with me then, now and forever.

MELINDA MILLER

Daddy Didn't Miss A Trick

Towards the end of my dad's physical days on earth, he was in the hospital preparing to release his spirit from his physical body. Most of the time he was in a coma-like state and we wondered if he heard us talking to him at all.

My mother, my sisters and my dad's brother, Uncle Normie, all visited him, yet, we wondered. When Uncle Normie visited he brought a Bible, and we all recited Psalm 23 from the Bible over my dad. It was very comforting having our uncle there praying with us, as we encouraged my dad to let go and go to the Light. That it was okay to leave now.

A few days later Daddy was finally called back Home to God; however, he made sure to make me keenly aware of the fact that he did know about everything that went on in his hospital room regardless of his coma-like state of being.

How did my dad do this, you may be wondering? My dad's spirit visited me the same evening that he passed over. I was in a twilight state of sleep at the time of his visit, but I vividly recall his visit and all that he communicated to me, and I wrote it down as it was happening so I wouldn't forget.

Some of the many things my dad showed me in my mind's eye that night were: Uncle Normie walking down the corridor of the hospital with a Bible under his arm. Yet, how could my dad have seen Uncle Normie walking down the corridor, when he was lying in a coma-like state in his room, unless his spirit was in the corridor at the time?

Another hospital incident that Daddy's spirit relayed to me that evening was able to be confirmed the next day by my sister. Daddy played a conversation in my mind in which I heard my sister's voice say, "I think the weather in Florida is supposed to be nice right now."

The next morning I very excitedly called my sister and told her about Daddy's spirit visiting me. I inquired about the conversation about the weather Florida I heard in my mind concerning her voice. My sister was shocked! She said, "When I was alone in Daddy's hospital room, and he seemed out of it, I was whispering on the phone with our cousin Jeanne. I was telling her about a possible a trip to Florida, and I said those very same words!"

So you see, Daddy didn't miss a trick!

This encounter with my dad's spirit, only a few hours after he passed over, enabled my heart's sorrow to be replaced with overflowing joy, as well as anticipation of more visits to come.

So much so, that I actually felt euphoric on the day of my dad's funeral service. I could not stop smiling because I knew my dad was not in that casket—only his discarded shell of a body that he no longer needed. I knew that my dad's spirit was free now and flying all around the room. I knew Daddy was enjoying all the conversations at his funeral and was relishing being there with his friends and family. And I was so happy for him and for me!

To validate my personal belief that Daddy was at his own funeral, that same evening he visited me again during the middle of the night, and showed me visions of scenes from his funeral and the subsequent luncheon in his honor.

I had the understanding that Daddy was going to be an even bigger part of my life than ever, now that he could travel with me to places his sick and frail body was unable to go before. So now I often invite him to come along with me to places, and he does! Most often he lets me know he is there by a distinctive trademark sign of his—massaging the top of my head! Daddy lives on and so does the ongoing loving relationship we had. A continuation of loving relationships exists for every one of God's children, no matter what side of the spiritual veil we reside. Thank You, dear Father and Jesus, for allowing all of this!

CHRISTINE DUMINIAK

* * *

CHAPTER 11

Computers

In this age of cyberspace our loved ones in spirit seem to enjoy communicating through our computers. They do this to let us know they are around us, to give help when needed, and to amaze and delight us.

Who Sent This Email?

My sister Jacquie passed away on February 24, 2001. She was only thirty-one years old and left behind two children. Her daughter was ten years old at the time. Before Jacquie passed, she made me promise her that her daughter would not go to live with the ex-husband because he was into drugs. I told her I would do everything I could to keep her daughter safe.

After Jacquie passed, her ex-husband came with the police and took her daughter away from us to live with him. During this very emotional and unsettling time for my niece, she had developed emotional problems. Since she was not living with me, there was no way for me to know when she needed extra help, care, and my intercession. So I prayed about this situation and prayed for contact from my sister.

My prayers were answered when my sister Jacquie started communicating with me to let me know her daughter needed my help. I started to notice that, when there was a problem with her little girl that I needed to know about, my lights would start flickering. I would then get involved to help.

But my sister Jacquie did not just stop at flickering lights. No, she went on to bigger and better ways to get my attention. My sister started emailing me her very own picture as an attachment! It was spooky at first.

The emails I received would show that I had sent them to one of my friends, with a copy to myself, even though I never had sent them out! These emails, with Jacquie's picture attached, were being sent when I was at work around Christmas time and no one was at home at those times, or the emails would be sent during the night when everyone was asleep.

Still, I wanted to be sure that my sister Jacquie was really doing this from Heaven, so I said to Jacquie, "If you can really do this, I want to receive your picture for Christmas on my computer." Sure enough, on Christmas Day her picture showed up on my computer, as an answered validation to my question.

My sister has sent her picture to me on my computer not only to signal me when there were problems with her daughter, but also at other times just to say, "Hi," after I had been thinking about her quite a bit. I treasure these special contacts from her.

Also, I am so relieved to report that my niece was eventually taken away from her biological father and is now living very happily away from him.

KATHY POTAVIN

The Raiders

One morning, a little before 6 a.m., I woke up and heard this very deep, loud voice talking. At first I thought it was coming from my TV. Upon further inspection of the house, I noticed that there was a light coming from my son's computer screen. My son was away at the time.

I looked and realized that the voice I heard was coming from his computer's start-up program, which is about the Raiders' professional football team. However, when I went to bed that night, his computer was turned off! It was quite startling that the computer and this particular Raiders' program jump-started all by itself! And so loudly too!

But to add to this interesting story, I believe there was a reason for this. I had become very friendly with a woman who had lost her son to suicide. Her son has visited me a few times in dreams. I always consider these visits blessings from God. I recently found out that his favorite football team is the Raiders! Was this her son who turned on the computer to the Raiders program? I believe so. I believe he wanted to let his mom know he was having fun and to say, "Hello."

LAURI

Michael's Screen Name

My son James Michael, who has passed, sends me ADCs via our computer. Out of the blue his screen name on AOL will appear on the computer screen, instead of ours. This has happened many times. Recently, I had been praying for an ADC, and not long afterwards, my prayer was answered.

I had been working on the computer using AOL for a while and then I signed off. My screen name was left showing on the sign-on page, as it should have been. I came back to the computer a little while later, and lo and behold, Michael's screen name was now on the screen's sign-on page, instead of mine! No one, but no one, was there to do it. I was really taken aback by this.

So, I said to Michael, "I know you can hear me, so please put it back the way it was with my screen name showing." I also said, "OK, I'll give you a few minutes."

I left the room for a little bit and when I came back, I was amazed. My screen name was put back on the sign-on page! WOW! I got goosebumps. Of course, Michael knows that I'm at the computer a lot and that I would notice. How clever of him!

CARMEN & JAMES R. CREIGHTON

Bridge Over Troubled Water

At the time that Darrell was suddenly murdered, he was the love of my life. I still kept in touch with his parents even after twelve years had gone by after his death. Because I was close to them, one day I was helping Darrell's parents move out of their house. While there I became violently ill because it was just too much for me emotionally being in his house and in his room, even after all of these years. I was in a terrible state.

When I am at home, to calm myself, I like to play music. Our computer has a jukebox program and is set on "random" select, meaning you start it by choosing a song, and then the computer will randomly select all the songs after that.

On this moving day I was very upset, so when I got home, I played "I Will Remember You" by Sara McLaughlin. As I was listening to the song, I was missing Darrell very badly, so I said aloud to the empty room, "Darrell, if you can hear me, flick the light switch or something." Well at that moment the Sara McLaughlin song was ending and the next one that came on was my and Darrell's special song "Time In A Bottle," by Jim Croce.

I calmed right down, knowing Darrell was with me. I stopped crying and just listened to our song.

I have since tried many times to play that song "I Will Remember You" on random select to see if our song "Time In A Bottle" would again come up right afterwards, but it never has. Also, I have noticed that "Bridge Over Troubled Water" by Simon and Garfunkle has become a song of communication from Darrell to me, and I play that from time to time.

Well one time when my computer was set on random select, "Bridge Over Troubled Water" played over and over and over. Now, the computer program has two settings—random select and continuous play. Continuous play causes the program to go down the list playing a different song each time, not one song over and over. Random select plays songs in a mix-up order. But "Bridge over Troubled Water" played five times in a row before I finally shut the computer off! And neither setting would have caused that to happen!

In my mind, these incidents were strong examples of electrical manipulation through the computer, as well as an important message to me that my love Darrell is still with me, especially when I need him the most.

ANNE W. LONDON

Nintendo's Mario

I had a good friend named Jackie Harrison, who sadly passed away June 8, 2002, due to a drunk driving incident. I would like to share an encounter that I had with what I believe to have been her spirit. On the evening of June 7, 2002, which was a Friday, Jackie had called and asked me if it would be all right for her to come over and see my new home. I told her that I would love for her to visit, but I would rather that she waited for her dad to bring her over because I really didn't want her walking that long of a distance in the evening. So we decided that she should wait and try to get a ride to my house sometime later that weekend or early the next week.

Well, unfortunately, the very next day she was killed by a drunk driver while riding her bike with her sister, so she never did make it over as we had planned.

About two weeks after her death, I was playing my Nintendo 64 Mario game, and something strange would happen every time I would put my controller down, or even when I just stopped playing the game for a minute. The game character that I was playing would continue to move around the screen, as if I were still controlling him, when I wasn't! I was really confused as to why this was happening because I had never had this happen before. I assumed that my husband had done something to the Nintendo game to make it do this on its own. However, when I questioned him about it, he said that he hadn't played on the Nintendo 64 in a couple of months. So I really didn't think too much about it because it never happened again after that one day.

A couple weeks after this curious event, I was telling Jackie's mother Sue about it, and she remembered how "Mario" was Jackie's favorite game to play, and also how much she had wanted to come and see my new home. That's when we both realized that Jackie had probably come to visit me and decided to make her presence known by taking over my game controller. So I definitely believe in visits from spirits that have crossed over, because I believe this is what happened to me.

ANNA & SUSIE HARRISON (JACKIE'S MOM)

CHAPTER 12

Dreams From Adults

> Dreams seem to be the easiest way for people to receive spiritual visits from their loved ones, as well as an easy way for spirits to communicate with us. If you receive a comforting dream from a loved one, and if it seems vivid and real, please realize that you have been blessed with a spiritual visit.

There's Your Father!

After my dad crossed over to God, I missed him so. One night while sleeping, I dreamed that I was walking with someone. I don't recall who this person was, but suddenly the person I was walking with said, "Patti, there's your father!"

I turned to look, and sure enough, it *was* my father. I only saw his face only, not the rest of his body. He turned to look at me, and once he was completely facing me, he reached for my hand and said, "I love you, Patti." I responded with, "I love you too." And then he was gone. Just as quickly as he appeared, he disappeared. But I knew it was him! The face I saw was clearly his face! While still dreaming, I said to myself, "I just had an ADC!" Even during my dream state, I knew I had received an actual visit from my father.

PATTI

My Father's House Has Many Rooms

Several months after my mom passed over I had a wonderful, warm dream in which she was looking at a new house with my husband and me (my mom lived with us for many years).

Mom looked wonderful in this dream! She was so full of light, energy and health; it amazed me. She kept exclaiming, "Look at this room! It's huge! Bigger than my bedroom!" She kept urging me to follow her through this enormous house. With each room she wanted to show me, we had to walk up three steps. Each room was larger than the last and even more beautiful. Mom was so excited!

I was getting depressed and kept saying, "We can't afford this!" I could hear my husband's voice calmly saying, "Don't worry, the Father will take care of us." I asked, "Who's going to pay for this?" Again I kept hearing, "Don't worry, God will take care of everything."

I finally asked how much it was going to cost and found out the cost was in the millions. I kept hearing, "It's already paid for. Don't worry about it. The Father has provided!"

My mom kept saying, "Wait till you see the yard!" The "yard" was off a high deck area, as we were now ten stories up. I looked out and said, "We need to get a fence for the dogs." Mom said, "Don't worry. They won't run away." I looked out and for miles saw an unending garden of trees and green grass.

After I woke up, I thought about this dream and came to the following conclusions:

Mom wanted me to know that she was alive, happy, healthy, and that the bonds of love I share with her can never be untied.

The house represented the passage in the Bible: "My Father's house has many rooms . . . I have prepared a place for you." I didn't have to worry about money because someday this "house" will be mine too. By being told, "It's already paid for. Don't worry about it. The Father has provided!" meant that the Father has provided Heaven through Jesus paying the debt for our sins, by His dying on the cross for us.

The garden represented Heaven, for which there is no end. The three steps that I had to ascend to see each room represented the Father, the Son and the Holy Spirit. By having to go up, I had to go to Heaven to be in "His" house.

This dream made such an impression on me that I will never forget it.

MICKEY PASKO-POWELL

Angie's Gift

My cousin Angie and I were childhood friends and teen partners in pranks. We went to the same high school and had the same friends. She was popular and outgoing, and I was very shy at the time.

Angie became a model, but, sadly, was always unlucky in love and later unlucky in health. My dear cousin eventually passed of ovarian cancer.

Angie and I lived on opposite coasts, so as time went by, we lost touch. I did not hear about Angie's death until a few weeks afterwards. Because we lived so far apart, I would not have been able to attend her funeral services even if I knew about it at the time.

One Christmas season, as it was drawing close to Christmas Day, I dreamt of Angie. In this dream visit she wore a white blouse and black dress slacks. She gave me the biggest hug! She handed me a small box—a gift. That was Angie for you; she was always such a giving person.

I was so thrilled at her visit. I said, "So did you decide to come back to tell me the secrets of Heaven?" She laughed and I could read her thoughts, as they were "thick" in the air. She communicated this thought to me, "You never let it go, do you?" Angie was referring to my quest for spiritual secrets, which I had prayed to her to deliver to me.

The next day I telephoned her sister Jenny to tell her that Angie arrived in a dream at Christmas time to bring me a gift. I told her that Angie wore a white, dressy, long-sleeved blouse and black slacks.

My cousin Jenny said, "Ohhhh . . . that's what we dressed her in for her funeral." Jenny confirmed that the blouse was even long-sleeved—just as I had described it.

My cousin Jenny was thrilled to know that her sister Angie was very much alive in her spiritual body. We will live forever more . . . because of Christmas Day.

JENNY FLORES

A Dream 4 All

The night before Easter, my son was really struggling and having a hard time with his anxieties and frustrations that seem to continually disturb his peace of mind. I was especially worried about him on this particular night, so I wasn't able to sleep. I decided to get up and read until I became sleepy; eventually sleep did come.

I began dreaming of my sweet daddy (who is with God now). He and I were together in a large crowd and I just kept hugging Daddy. I was so happy and he was too.

As we walked through the crowd of people, Daddy was hugging some, shaking hands with others, and laughing with joy. He told me that he was fine and very happy. I begged him to stay. He told me that he couldn't stay but everything was fine. He was so happy! Well I was so glad to have dreamt of Daddy, as I have only dreamt of him twice since he went Home to God.

I woke up to a bright, beautiful Easter morning, and as usual, my mother and I sat on the front porch and drank coffee together. My mother was in a wonderful mood. She had gotten up early and brought out the pretty floral tablecloth and made the dining room so pretty for Easter.

As we sat there on the porch she smiled and said, "I dreamt of Daddy last night." You can imagine how excited I was! I said, "You're kidding! So did I!" Her face lit up and she said, "He was here wasn't he?" Then she told me of her dream:

In her dream she was cold while she was trying to sleep, and my daddy came over to her and covered her up with a blanket. She was so very happy to see him and that he did this for her! When she woke up she had on an extra blanket! This dream has given her some peace because now she feels that Daddy loves and forgives her for any real or imagined pain that she may have caused him.

Then in the afternoon we were preparing our Easter dinner, when I decided to put the eggshells down the garbage disposal. Well the sink stopped up, and there I was on Easter Sunday with the plunger, plunging the sink! I worked on that sink for one hour, to no avail.

My daughter arrived to share dinner with us, and I asked her if she would like to ride to the store with me to get some Liquid Plumber. On the drive over there I casually mentioned that her grandma and I both dreamt of her papa the night before. Well, you should have seen the look on her face! You guessed it. She dreamt of him as well! I was smiling from ear-to-ear after hearing her news.

Because three of us had dreamt of Daddy, after we got home from the store I just had to ask my son if he had any dreams the night before. He said, "As a matter of fact I dreamt of Papa last night!" All four of us! Can you believe it?

Later in the evening I drove to my daughter's house after dinner. As I turned on the radio the song "We Are Family" was playing. Now on any other day this song would not have any special significance, but you see, my daddy has a sister, a brother, one of his sons and his parents with him in Heaven. Part of the lyrics has to do with walking together as we come on by. These words, of course, took on great meaning as a confirmation to me that my daddy's family members are with him, as they come on by to visit us.

Thank You, Jesus! What a wonderful gift! Thank You, God! I love You!

I lift Him up and praise His holy name. Thank you, Jesus, for with You all things are possible. To God I give the glory for these precious signs from above.

SHEILA SHEPHERD

* * *

AFTER-DEATH COMMUNICATIONS

CHAPTER 13

Dreams From Children

There is probably nothing more healing and comforting than receiving a dream visit from the spirits of our children who have left earth early to return back Home with God. They come to show us how happy they are but, also, want us to be happy for them too.

Harley & Baby Harley's Visit

On July 22, 2000, our son Harley was just twelve days shy of turning twenty-one when he was killed in an automobile accident. He failed to negotiate a turn shortly after midnight and struck a tree. His car instantly caught fire. We had no positive identification for his body for three days, but we knew it was our Harley. The loss of our son has been incredibly difficult for me, my wife, and the rest of our family.

The day before Harley's funeral, his girlfriend Kristi went into labor at 3 a.m. on July 25. My wife and our two daughters went to the hospital, and I stayed home to answer phone calls, etc. I started to pray . . . crying with grief. I prayed for the safety of Kristi and her baby, and I prayed for our son.

It is hard for me to put into words the pain I felt. I then fell asleep. The incredible dream I had was one that has changed my life. I can tell you the dream was unlike most dreams I have had before. I usually don't remember them and most of the time they make no sense, except this dream was so moving and real, that I was able to remember all of it.

The dream: I was in a room floating about five feet directly above my son Harley, as he was lying face-up in a hospital bed. I don't recall anything but his smiling face, a feeling that he was doing fine, and that everything was going to be okay. He looked very peaceful and I remember calling out his name, "Harley . . . Harley . . . Harley," with a feeling of joy that here was my boy and he was okay. The look on his face was one of happiness. I never spoke a word, though. The communication was all through thought.

Then all of a sudden I recall being distracted to my right for just a millisecond, and I remember this bright intense light like no other I have ever seen before. The room filled with this bright light. I looked back at the bed, and Harley was still lying down, but now with his back towards me. As Harley rolled over to face me, it was no longer Harley. It was now a different male—the same age as Harley—twenty years old, but he was not Harley! The more I gazed into his eyes, I realized this other male looked a lot like Harley, but he was *not* Harley. I again remember saying Harley's name a couple of times. I was still saying Harley's name to this new person, even though this male only resembled Harley. Then I remember being drawn out of the room, like being pulled away like a vacuum was sucking me right out of the room.

I next awoke in my bed . . . eyes wide open with this sense of a gift being given to me to see my son and to know that he was okay. I felt as if I had been on a very long journey. I was filled with joy like I have never known before. I wanted to be sorrowful for him, but I just couldn't because I was so happy for him! I felt complete joy and happiness. I then wanted to call my wife Debbie and tell her what had just happened.

Before I could, the phone rang and it was Debbie. I told her what I had just experienced. She cried tears of joy and happiness with me over this dream visitation. Later on that day, our grandson Harley Peter Jr. was born at 3 p.m. I went to the hospital to visit my grandson for the very first time. As I looked at his face I was struck with awe—baby Harley was the second male face I had seen in my dream—the one that wasn't Harley's, but resembled him! Well here he was staring me in the eye . . . it was my grandson. The face in my dream looked just like my new grandson, but now twenty years younger. I remember saying to Harley Jr., "Welcome, didn't we just meet not too long ago?" Little Harley was always going to be named Kade. However, after Harley died, Kristi, Harley's girlfriend, decided to name him Harley, after his father.

Prior to that dream visit, I was not aware of such things as after-death communications (ADCs). Since that first dream visit, I could add a lot to that ADC, mostly about how spiritual and uplifting it has been to me personally. It's something that was real, as real as my living and breathing. I believe it was a vision to help me feel happiness, joy, and such a sense of peace and love. I felt it was also for my understanding concerning certain things that would happen in my life. I thank GOD for my life. I know how precious it really is. I know I can make a difference with my actions. We were blessed to have been given a grandson. I have spoken with many who have nothing to remember a lost loved one by, but we have Harley's son now.

Our son's loss has been the most difficult thing I have ever had to overcome. I didn't know one could hurt that much . . . and still there are no words to describe it. It is a sense of loss that we wish would go away, but won't. I have grieved many times since Harley's death, but I know he is in a much better place, and that he is with us more now than he ever was before his death. Our salvation in all of this is our faith in Jesus and that we all will be one again.

JEFF & DEBBIE FRANK

A Guided Tour of Heaven

When I was pregnant with my fourth child Julia, who was to be my first daughter after having three sons, I went into preterm labor after only twenty-three weeks of pregnancy. Julia was born and lived for only one hour and died in my arms. I felt a very special connection to my precious baby girl and she has changed my life forever for the better. She was my angel.

After this immensely strong but brief bonding with Julia, I had prayed for months after this loss to have some kind of spiritual contact with her. However, after patiently waiting, I felt that I might never be able to see her or talk to her spirit in this lifetime. Although I have felt her presence nearby, I desired more. I desired to dream of her. One night, when I was least expecting it, I had a dream, which I now feel in my heart-of-hearts was a dream visit with my beautiful baby girl Julia.

The dream started out with my walking up a dark stairway, and when I got to the light at the top, I was greeted by the most precious little girl with brown hair that curled at the ends and who was about the age of two years old. She was just the most angelic little thing. I immediately reached out for her precious little hand and helped her to walk. We walked the streets and were introducing ourselves to many people. I was so proud of my little girl. It was a definite mother-daughter feeling I was experiencing,

This dream visit from her has left a song in my heart. I know that I was blessed to have been taken to Heaven in order to meet and spend time with my little girl Julia. I feel so blessed by God and thankful for allowing me to break the barriers of this life and Heaven in order to have a very special visit with my precious child.

TRACI AND JULIA

Humor and Laughter

Our son John B. Murtaugh was born on April 2, 1975. At the moment he was placed into our arms, we knew that our family was complete. He had become our world.

Sadly, John was stricken with juvenile diabetes at the age of two, and he carried this disease until his crossing over to God on August 24, 2000, at age twenty-five. The disease inflicted his life with seizures, laser eye surgeries, and over the years the daily shots he had to endure, totaled thirty thousand. The disease never hindered John's dream of graduating from college as a Computer Engineer. He graduated on May 5, 2000, just months before his passing. The smile he had on his face that day will be burned into our thoughts forever. Oh how he held that degree so high for all to see as he crossed the stage of his university. We were so proud of his accomplishment, especially so, because of all his physical afflictions.

A month before John crossed, he had nightly dreams of flying like a bird over rivers and valleys. He would wake and just talk and talk about it. His beautiful blue eyes sparkled with such thoughts of being able to fly. Maybe it was the Lord's way of preparing this precious spirit for a new world?

Throughout my life, I expected death of the elderly and I expected grief. However, the profound grief we experienced, when our son John passed away, was unbearable. As his mother, I began my search for him in the afterlife. The afterlife was never a thought that I had ever considered before John's passing, much less the concept that my son would have the ability to communicate with me. However, with God's blessing, our son John continues to be such a big part of our lives through many afterlife communications.

There have been dream visits to my husband Kev and me. What is such a blessing is that these visits have addressed a particular concern in our grief. For instance, Kev sorely missed John's laugh. So in the very first dream visit Kev received, he found himself in a room talking with John, and at the very end of the dream visit—he heard John laugh! Kev remembers it so vividly even today.

I, too, have had many dream visits. As an explanation of this next dream visit, I need to share that because of my overwhelming grief, I was unable to look at or say goodbye to John's lifeless body at the hospital or at the viewing and funeral; because of this, I had been carrying a lot of guilt.

I believe John arranged a special dream visit to me in a funeral type of a setting, so I could overcome my guilt by allowing me to see him happy now. In this dream visit I got to see John in the outdoors and cheerfully talking to a crowd of people—all the while sitting up in an open glass type of a box/casket!

I found my way through the crowd but could not get close, only close enough to see him. John suddenly laid down as if he were about to go somewhere. So before he left, I yelled, "I love you, Baby." And the crowd suddenly quieted as John teased me with his usual humorous style by playfully saying, "I like you too." Then he gave me one of his grins, and he finally said the words I longed to hear, "I LOVE YOU TOO."

This dream visit has been the most healing one of all for me because being a part of this happy scenario of John's funeral, where I got to tell him that I love him, replaced my guilt and regrets with an inner peace and a sense of completion.

CATHYJMF & KEV MURTAUGH

He Reunited Us From Beyond

My son John was the funniest, nuttiest kid you could ever meet. He loved his family so and would do anything for us. When he was thirty-one, he passed suddenly from myocarditis. We believe this happened during the night while sleeping.

Myocarditis is a virus that destroys the heart. It is a deadly, silent one that, by the time it shows its symptoms, it can be too little too late. Only days before John passed, he was a seemingly healthy young man with a brand new baby girl, Kallie, who was born on March 27, 2002. John passed the beginning of June, a little more than two months after his daughter was born.

Before John passed, he was out at a work site, where he worked with bulldozers and such on building roads. John took off from work in time for his baby Kallie to be born. After he returned to work he was extremely tired, so much so, that when he was home he did not even have the strength to lift up his newborn baby. So John went to see a doctor. The doctor misdiagnosed him, for he said that maybe John had hepatitis, but to go on back to work anyway, and they would get him the results of the blood work when the results came back.

John went back to work, but two days later I talked to him. He said, "Mom, I am so tired. I will talk to you about the girls later." I never knew what that meant. I assumed he meant he wanted to talk about the possibility of having exposed all the girls in our family to hepatitis, if that was what he had. He died early the next morning. He never moved in his sleep.

After his funeral, his wife threw me out of her and little baby Kallie's life. Her reason was that I saw my son's body before she (his wife) did. A second reason she gave was because she didn't want anything to do with John's sister. This reasoning made no sense at all, and I was crushed that I was no longer going to be allowed to see my new granddaughter Kallie. Not only had I lost my son, but now I had another unexpected loss—baby Kallie. I was further devastated.

This had been John's second marriage. I hadn't kept in close touch with John's first, Carrie, although I loved her dearly. Carrie and John had a son together, Ryan, my grandson who I didn't get to see very often. However, at John's funeral, Carrie brought Ryan to the funeral too. I was thrilled to see him, and Carrie was so nice to me. She kept asking me if I was all right.

Sometime later, Carrie had an ADC visit from John. She did not even know what to call it, or even if she should tell me. She wasn't sure if she was asleep or awake, but she felt like she was awake at the time. In this visit, John called her to pick him up at a cabin, a place she had never seen or been to before. Carrie drove down a winding dirt road to the cabin, and John came over to the pickup she was driving. He got in and immediately laid his head in her lap. He said, "Carrie, I am so tired, just so tired." Then he closed his eyes. She had the feeling that if she could get him to hold on just long enough to get him to the cabin he would last. She kissed him on his head and he left. Carrie never knew about how physically tired John was at the end, nor had she known about the circumstances surrounding his passing, so, you see, he told her this news in his dream visit.

When Carrie shared John's spiritual visit with me, I remembered that our family used to go to a cabin in New Mexico. This cabin was very similar to the one Carrie described to me that was in her dream.

Ever since this visit to Carrie from John's spirit, she and I have been very close and it rekindled our love for one another. She and her husband came to my daughter's rehearsal and wedding, and her husband even helped in important ways at the wedding too.

I believe one of the reasons why John visited Carrie was to reunite us and help replace my devastating losses. Even though I know one grandchild can never replace another, it helped my heart to have Ryan, my precious grandson, as well as Carrie and her husband in my life.

John's gravestone says, "Always there when needed," and truer words were never written.

MONA

Moving On

We lost our son Harley in a car accident on July 22, 2000. His son, our grandson, Little Harley was born the day before his funeral.

It has been very tough on our whole family and his girlfriend Kristi, but we have all moved on with our lives the best we can over the years. Life is once again looking up.

Three years after Harley's passing, I had a very special dream. In this dream I was just one of many people walking through a crowded area when all of a sudden I saw our son Harley. In previous dreams where I have seen him, I have always been surprised and overwhelmed at the sight of him.

This time was different. I saw him and just sort of casually went about my business of walking around and taking in everything that was going on in my surroundings.

Shortly afterwards, I saw Harley's girlfriend Kristi walking around with a male companion. I didn't recognize him. It was at this time that I noticed Harley walk up to Kristi and hold onto her arm and hold her tight with his head on her shoulder. The male companion seemed to be at ease with this and stepped aside, as all three of them just stood there smiling. I didn't think anything about it and kept on watching them and then decided it was time to move on.

I turned and started walking away wondering if I should say anything like "goodbye." It was at that time that I turned and said, "Seeya, Harley!" He turned to me and gave me the biggest smile, all the while he had his head on Kristi's shoulder and seemed very happy.

With that said, Kristi has struggled with moving on. She has recently started seeing a fellow named Dusty, whom I had only met one time. It was a very brief meeting and I basically said, "Hi!" and they left our house after Kristi had picked up Little Harley.

The day after my dream, Little Harley came to stay with us overnight. The next day Kristi came to the house to pick up Little Harley and I caught a glimpse of Dusty sitting in the car waiting for her. I went outside and said, "Hi!" to Dusty and had a chat with him. I noticed throughout our conversation that he really resembled our son Harley in his mannerisms, and in how polite, well-mannered, and caring he was throughout our talk. Needless to say, I immediately took a big liking to him.

When Little Harley and Kristi were leaving our house and got to the car, I told Kristi we could watch Little Harley for a few more hours, if they wanted to enjoy the beautiful day. Kristi asked Harley if he wanted to go with her or stay at Grandpa and Grandma's house, and he said he wanted to stay with Grandpa—which made me feel great, of course!

A few hours later, they stopped back and picked up Little Harley, and once again, I felt that Dusty was a super guy and that he may be the one for Kristi.

After they left, I told my wife Debbie about my dream, and it was then that I started to feel that my dream was some sort a of message that our son Harley was very pleased with Dusty. I cannot remember the other fellow's face in the dream but am confident that it had everything to do with Dusty, as well as our son Harley's approval of him.

The timing of it all—the dream and getting a chance to really know Dusty a little better the very next day—was incredibly comforting to my wife and me. I really feel for the first time that Kristi may have found somebody she can spend the rest of her life with.

JEFF AND DEBBIE FRANK

* * *

AFTER-DEATH COMMUNICATIONS

* * *

CHAPTER 14

Electrical

The spirits of our loved ones seem to enjoy communicating with us by tinkering with electrical devices. God must get quite a chuckle out of these ADCs!

Who Turned on the Ceiling Fan?

I lost my mom (my best friend) to advanced breast cancer. It was wintertime, and eleven months had gone by since her passing. The first anniversary of my mom's going Home to God was almost upon us, and I had been thinking about her a lot because of the upcoming anniversary. I had been praying to God about it, and I also had been asking my mom to send me a sign that she was with me.

I believe that my prayers were answered soon thereafter. My hubby, son and I were all in the dining room where we have a combination ceiling fan/light fixture. I was walking out of the dining room when my hubby suddenly blurted out, "Wow the ceiling fan is starting up by itself!" I turned and watched the fan accelerate from slow to medium, and it stayed on steadily and smoothly continuing to turn at medium speed. We had the lights on that were attached to the fan, but the fan's pull-chain hadn't been touched, for we only use it in the summertime!

I said, "Ohhhhh, I think my mom is here." My young son then added, "Yea, Grandma!" My hubby got up on a chair to inspect the fan because he couldn't figure out how the fan turned on all by itself. Now here is the supernatural part—My hubby said, "Oh my God, the chain is in the OFF position!"

The fan was spinning on medium speed, but the switch for the fan, which is separate from the light switch, was OFF! My hubby proceeded to pull the chain three times, and then it did finally shut off. I asked my hubby if it were possible for the fan to just start up by itself while being in the OFF position? My hubby was just as perplexed as I was and answered, "I don't know how this happened!"

This is the same light/fan fixture that the light part switched on by itself four months ago. At that time, I was crying and lit a candle for my mom and grandma's souls and asked for a sign. I came back into the room a little later and was talking to my little boy, who was sitting in the dark watching TV. While I was talking to him, the light switch on the wall in the dining room suddenly flipped up all by itself and the light came on! My little boy ran out of the house from being so startled!

After these two incidents concerning the same light/fan fixture, I realized that Mom was using this electrical fixture as a way of communicating with me to let me know she hears me and is with me.

Both events occurred after I prayed really hard and begged Mom for a sign. Other than that, nothing unusual with the switch or light/fan has ever occurred the whole six years we have lived here.

JEANNE MARIE

My Special Touch Lamp

One Christmas I gave my father the most beautiful handcrafted wreath. To my surprise he was repulsed by it and kept it hanging in the closet. He said it reminded him of the wreaths that were thrown out to sea when there was a burial. He was retired from the U.S. Navy.

It was then that I first realized my dad was afraid of death.

By Christmas 1998, my father's health had diminished to one of frailty. He could no longer speak and communicated silently by blinking his eyes. I felt so sorry for him. His two brothers arrived for this holiday from northern California to see my father, who was their eldest brother. While here, they went on and on about where Dad should die right in front of him. I just watched in amazement of how openly they spoke to Dad about this, since they hadn't seen him in a couple of years, and I was concerned about Dad's fears.

I entered his room with my daughter and said, "Daddy, don't be afraid of death. Jesus Christ died so you would live forever. Nobody dies. You will live forever. When you get to the other side, your mother and father and family will be waiting for you." He began to weep, and it was in total silence, as his little face wrinkled up and his eyes were so sorrowful. My daughter, who was about seventeen years old, saw her grandpa crying and said, "Stop it, Mommy! You're making him cry!" She hugged him so tightly and said, "Oh, Grandpa, don't cry. You will never die. Jesus promised us that you would live."

Three weeks later, he passed over in the hospital. I went to his body and whispered in his ear, "Dad, visit me in my dreams and let me know you're okay."

The third day after Dad was buried I was asleep and I opened up my eyes. The instant my eyes opened, the touch lamp beside our bed lit up to the highest setting! I screamed in delight, "Hello Daddy! God bless you! I love you!"

It was the first of many times my father would communicate with me from the afterlife. Daily, the instant I would open my eyes and then look at the lamp, my father would turn on the lamp automatically for me! Dad was messaging me: "The moment you open your eyes to this world, your loved ones are with you in the journey."

Now my husband Kendall was not a believer of these heavenly visits. Kendall would laugh at how I greeted my father. One morning Kendall asked me to turn the lamp off because the light was bothering him. As I started to lift my arm to reach over Kendall to turn the lamp off, my father did not allow me to do this. Before I even got near the lamp, my dad's spirit turned the lamp right off. The message was: "Your loved ones will help you."

This touch lamp really had me going. I would cross from room to room and peek in to see if it was lit. One day out of frustration due to life's trials and tribulations, I walked into the room and blurted, "Daaaaaaad, I need a friend!" As soon as these words came out of my mouth, the touch lamp lit up! I jumped back in surprise and said, "Okay, Dad, I have a friend in you." I took this to be my dad's message: "You are never alone. We have friends in Heaven—in very high places."

Since Dad was messaging me so much through the touch .amp, I decided to write on a piece of paper the codes my dad and I were using. The touch lamp would light up in three settings of low, medium and high. The codes were as follow:

Low = I love you.

Medium = Warning . . . warning . . . I am protecting you.

High = Everything is going to be okay!

At other times he would zoom all the light settings at once, over and over. It was as if he were telling a story. I loved it when he did that.

One day I remembered that before my dad passed and he was living with me, he watched as I danced all around in the living room. It made him laugh so much, and all in silence, because he could no longer speak.

So with this memory of my dad in my mind, I went to the touch lamp and said, "Hey, Dad, want to see me dance for you?" I began to dance slowly turning around and singing something like, "I'm dancing for my father." He orchestrated the lighting as if he were twinkling it on and off. I asked him to hold on, and I went to get my brother. My brother, who was too afraid to enter the room, stayed at the doorway and I began to dance to the lighting. When I stopped–the lighting would stop. When I would continue–the lighting, zooming from level to level, would continue too.

I motioned for my brother to come into the room, but he wouldn't. He was amazed. He said, "Jenny, I heard you talk about this. I never thought I would see anything like this! This is amazing."

Sure it was. What lamp stops lighting up when you stop and when you tell it to continue, it does?

JENNY FLORES

Magical Streetlights

My story of uncanny streetlight disruptions began within weeks after my twenty-four-year-old son Jason passed over in the summer of 1999. His unexpected passing left each one of his family members and friends in the midst of our own personal and grievous blackout.

Jason was an energetic, lively, charismatic individual but it never occurred to us that even after the finality of his death, he could possibly make an attempt to connect with me from the other side through the electrical energy of streetlights.

On a particularly clear summer night, when my grief was still new and the sky was filled with bright stars, I sadly drifted outside from my kitchen with a cup of tea to look at the stars and moon and to cry out silently from my heart at the reasons and reality of my devastating grief. A mother never expects to outlive her child. It's the unspoken word that we pray will never take place in our lifetime.

I suddenly noticed that the streetlight by my driveway began flickering. I initially thought the bulb inside may need replacing. It never occurred to me that it could possibly be my son's spirit letting me know he was there listening to my sorrows and had indeed survived the black hole we call death. At that point in time, I honestly never heard of ADCs but always held the belief that spirits live on after transitioning to the other side. Before I stepped back inside my home that night, the streetlight had returned to its full intensity of brightness.

Another week passed, and I returned outside to view the beautiful night sky and reflect upon the profound absence of my handsome son in my life. The same streetlight started another captivating repertoire of flickering, blackening out, returning to a dim light, and then slowly back to full brightness. I intently gazed at the streetlight in awe, and my first gut reaction was that this was much too coincidental. It was at that very moment it all connected for me! My senses rationalized that it must be my precious Jason's loving energy coming through that streetlight! The happiness and joy that swiftly coursed through my body was extraordinarily mystical.

In the months and years that followed, I began to witness certain streetlights repeating the same predictable patterns. As I would walk the quiet streets at night by the places significant in the life and memory of my son (whether it's the streetlight by his former elementary school; nearby his best friend's house; by the memorial garden plot in our town honoring his name; the streetlight on the corner of our street, or by our driveway), the timing was incredibly perfect as the streetlights would react as I passed by. It's during those wondrous moments I take the opportunity to say "Hello" to my son and warmly welcome the precious time he bestows upon me, with God's loving encouragement, to visit me from the spirit world.

There are also times, whether I'm sitting outdoors or quietly at home that I'll have a meditative moment of conversation to my son, when suddenly I'm aware that the streetlight, located just outside my window by our driveway, goes out and comes back on in its usual pattern of signaling.

It always thrills and delights me because, to the awakening of my keen senses, I believe it's my beautiful son's acknowledgment of his spiritual presence to comfort and enchant me. I still continue to this day to feel dearly loved by him. It's always a very special reunion for us both, through the bonds of mother and child, that we are continually blessed by God to gloriously and eternally connect by the sheer magnitude of never-ending love.

HELEN

Reading With My Dad

My father Stanley was diagnosed with pancreatic cancer on June 13,1994, at age sixty-five. We had five months to say goodbye to a very vibrant, loving, and dynamic man. It was so very difficult, especially because we did not discuss his impending death during those five months—just loving recollections of happier times and Dad's comfort. However, five days prior to his passing, Dad finally did speak of his inevitable passing when he made a request regarding his funeral to the grown children in the family at his bedside. Also, he referred to visiting from the afterlife by telling my daughter Shannon that, if he could, he will be "on her shoulder" in spirit.

After my father passed on November 17, 1994 there were electrical visits from him. The light at my bedside would flicker most nights when I read before going to sleep. There had been no problem with this lamp prior to his passing, and it continued to flicker even when the light bulb was replaced with a new one. At first the flickering would repeat itself about six times in the one to two hours I would be reading before I went to sleep. This lasted for about six weeks. Then, gradually, it would only flicker once or twice a night, and then about once a week, up until about five to six months after his passing. I had a very strong sense and a knowing that my dad was communicating with me during these times.

Except for one other ADC I received at Christmas time, I had no other signs from my father that I recognized until my birthday on June 3, 1995.

My watch needed to be cleaned by the jeweler, as it had stopped running. I decided to drop it off for repair on my birthday. After coming back home, I thought perhaps the jewelers would want the paperwork that came with the watch. So I searched for the paperwork that same day—my birthday, June 3. Much to my surprise, when I found the box the watch had come in, there was a note in my father's handwriting that read, "Dear Carol, I hope this June 3 will be a special day for you. Happy Birthday and we sure love you. Love, Mom and Dad." This was dated Tuesday a.m., May 30, 1989.

I had forgotten all about that note written six years earlier . . . and forgotten that I had even saved it! I felt that my dad had directed me to that note on my special day because he wanted to wish me a Happy Birthday. It made my day! A very special birthday wish, indeed. All I could do was look up right at my father's picture and say, "Thank you, Dad."

CAROL

A Mother's Love

My mother had been ill. She was a long time chronic insulin dependent diabetic–very noncompliant most of the time. Her friend called me one day and said, "Your Mom says she wishes her little girl were here." I immediately knew something was wrong. I got in my truck and drove from Texas to Oklahoma, where she lived.

When I walked in the door she was lying on the couch. I couldn't believe how she looked! In the three weeks since I had seen her last, she must have lost thirty pounds. She looked awful! She looked like she was dying. My mind immediately rejected that thought, though. I put her in my truck and drove back to Texas–determined to get her better medical care and to have her close to me, so I could look after her.

By the time we got there, she was looking so badly that I just went straight to the ER and checked her in. After many tests it was determined she was in a mild ketoacidosis, was suffering from gastroparesis–which can be devastating for a diabetic–and had an intestinal bacteria, commonly referred to by us in the medical field, as C. diff. She was going to be admitted into the hospital. It was very late, and I still needed to call my brother and let him know what was going on, so Mom said I should go ahead and go on home.

I was hesitant, but because I was so tired, I agreed. As I was getting ready to leave I reached down and kissed her forehead. She held my arm for a moment and said, "Love each other." She was referring to my brother and me because we sometimes were at odds over things, usually regarding my mother. I assured her I loved my brother, and always would (thinking to myself the whole time, what an odd thing for her to say). It wasn't like her to be so serious; she was the one to joke everything away. I left the ER confident she would be well taken care of, and that she was not critically ill. I got home, called my brother, and then went to bed. It was past 1 a.m. by this time.

About 5 a.m. the hospital called and woke me from sleep. "Your mother has taken a turn for the worse. You better come down to the hospital." I was frantic. I drove to the hospital and went straight to ICU where they had taken her. They hadn't even gotten her into the ICU bed, and were performing CPR. She was hooked up to a ventilator and a heart monitor. The doctor who was present was one I knew and worked with frequently. He came and told me that nothing was working. She apparently had a sudden heart attack. He said I could go in and see her and to see if my talking to her would help.

I walked into the room. I looked at her for the first time since I left her there at the hospital. It was obvious she was no longer there, but had passed over. Her pupils were fixed and dilated. There was no activity of her own on the heart monitor, only that which was being induced artificially. I bent down, anyway, close to her ear. I hugged her and cried. I begged her not to leave me. I told her how much I loved her. But there was no response, not from her outward physical body anyway.

Then, suddenly, everyone in the room noticed the heart monitor's sudden activity! The monitor now indicated a heart rate and a blood pressure, but there were no signs of life by looking at her! I continued to talk to her. Amazingly, for about five to ten minutes this unexplained activity with the heart monitor continued. Then, just as suddenly, it stopped!

During this time the ICU nurses were attempting to obtain pulses and blood pressure manually, with no success. The doctor asked me what I wanted them to do; he felt there was no chance of resuscitation. I agreed and told them to stop. I knew she did not want to have CPR or the artificial breathing apparatus; we had talked about that before. I knew these were her wishes. I felt that this was what she was asking of me.

I left the room, the doctor followed me and said, "That was the only time since this started that she maintained any steady heart rate and blood pressure!" He obviously was very amazed. I heard his words but was in too much pain for it to register much at the time. My world had just ended, and at the time, I felt as if I had killed her and was responsible for her death. It took me awhile to get past that.

That was my first communication from Mom after she had passed, which was in the presence of ICU nurses and a well-known and respected doctor. There was no way the facts could be refuted. Mom stuck around the hospital knowing I would be there, knowing I would be devastated. She tried to communicate in the only way she could at that moment, to let me know that she lives on and still hears me and is with me.

PATRICIA VASQUEZ

* * *

AFTER-DEATH COMMUNICATIONS

* * *

CHAPTER 15

Forgiveness

Forgiveness is a Divine virtue available to humans. The Godly act of forgiving frees us from the burdens of guilt and anger. It is never too late to forgive or be forgiven because our loved ones still hear us!

Brian's Murder

I was just an average wife and mother of three. Our youngest son Brian had just turned nineteen and was the only one still living at home. On June 24, 1989 Brian went out with an acquaintance from our neighborhood. Brian didn't usually pal around with this fellow even though he knew him. Because I always had a very bad feeling about this particular person, I really didn't want Brian going out with him. Brian told me not to worry, though, and that they were going to a carnival. He said that he would be home early, gave me a big hug, and said, "I love you." Those were to be the last words that he ever said to me.

When Brian was still not home by midnight, I got up from my bed and started looking out the windows, hoping to see or hear the car. I climbed back into bed fifteen minutes later, said a prayer that Brian would be okay, and then dozed off.

I started dreaming that Brian and I were at Disney World on our favorite ride "It's A Small World." We were really having a good time. The ride stopped and we both got off, and then Brian starting walking away from me. As he walked away I saw two women, whose faces I could not see, dressed in long white dresses. Each one was walking alongside of Brian. He never looked back.

I suddenly awoke as though a bolt of electricity shot through my body. I sat up and looked at the clock, it was 1 a.m. on June 25. I had a very sick feeling that something had happened to Brian. Were those women actually angels escorting Brian to Heaven? Was God preparing me for what was about to happen in our lives? Looking back, I believe that is what happened.

The next morning two policemen came to our door. They told us that they wanted us to go and see our son Brian, who was in the hospital. Although they knew Brian had already passed, they wanted to wait till we got to the hospital to be given the devastating news—that Brian had been murdered.

Upon hearing the heartbreaking news that would change my world forever, I instinctively knew that the acquaintance, who had been out with Brian the night before, had murdered my son.

Two "coincidences" happened, which I attribute to Brian's spirit. When we received the death certificate, it showed 1 a.m., June 25 to be the time of Brian's passing. This was the exact time that I felt the bolt of electricity in my body and sat up in bed.

Also, the following Sunday, my husband Duane and I were in bed and the phone rang at 7:30 a.m. When I picked up the receiver, I only heard loud static. As the static quieted down, a tremendous warm, peaceful feeling came over me. I then remembered that Brian's body was found at 7:30 a.m. the Sunday before. I also remembered saying a prayer at Brian's funeral for God to give me a sign that Brian was okay. I truly believe that this was the sign I prayed for.

A few months later I dreamt that Brian was in the kitchen and we were talking. He told me that he had died because his head was hurting him. (His head had been bashed with a blunt instrument, so much so that when his body was found, half his head was gone.)

In the dream Brian told me that he loved me but also loved where he was now. He said, "Come with me and I will take you there." He took my hand, and in a flash, we were in the most beautiful place. Everything there was all white, except for the brilliant colors of the flowers. In the distance there was a building which looked like a church; to its left was a white footbridge. I didn't see anyone else but Brian, but sensed that there were a lot of people on the other side of the bridge. I wanted to cross over the bridge, but Brian said, "No, it's not your time." Brian told me that he was very happy there, and the only thing that made him sad was seeing us cry. He told me that we would be together someday but until then to be happy for him.

I was very angry when I woke up because I still wanted to be with Brian. Brian and I were very close. However, that special dream has given me some peace over time. I believe I was shown what Heaven looks like. It was so beautiful and peaceful, and you could just feel the overwhelming love there!

We went public with our story in order to obtain justice and the protection we felt we needed because the murderer was still loose and harassing us. After that, strange things started happening in our house.

A lamp in our living room would snap on and off by itself. When the television was on, it would flip through the stations by itself, the way Brian use to channel surf. Books even starting flying off the bookshelves! I own hundreds of books, yet only the same three books would fly off the shelf time and again. These three books all have titles having to do with death, justice, and the afterlife. I even put these three books in different rooms, yet, the same three would still end up across the room on the floor. It was almost as if Brian were giving us messages! After a long struggle for justice, Brian's murderer admitted his guilt and was convicted.

Only someone who has lost someone to murder would know the hate, rage, anger and pain that you experience. Yet, I didn't want hate and anger to run my life. So I prayed very hard to God for His help and direction. I ended up starting and running the group Parents of Murdered Children, but my real healing began when God led me to the prison system. There I confronted men who had murdered and really made them understand how the victims' families were impacted. I found that I didn't hate these men, only their deeds, and I still remain in contact with them today.

Over the years, between Brian's birthday on May 1 and the anniversary of his passing on June 25, we always get signs from Brian. The television will start surfing channels all by itself, or the TV will be on, and suddenly it will just turn itself off. We have noticed that positive events always happen between these dates every year too.

I truly believe that, if we ask God to be with us in our darkest hours, He will see us through anything. It was my deep faith in God that got me through this tragedy. Although I will never get over the pain of losing Brian, feeling Brian's presence all the time comforts me. I know that he is with God and someday I will see and be with him once again. Until that day comes, I will try to be the best person I can be and try to make positive things out of negative situations.

PHYLLIS HOTCHKISS

Kujo Asked for Forgiveness

I had taken in an elderly, blind dog. I had Lucky for several months, and it just broke my heart to have to finally put him down. I missed him so much, even though I had two other dogs. Not long after Lucky crossed over, I had a vivid dream. In this dream, there was Lucky running with his tail wagging, licking my face and telling me how much he loved me and was grateful that I had cared for him during his last days.

Also in the dream there was another dog that I used to have, whose name was Murphy. I also had to have Murphy put down after seven years, because he acted like Kujo and had attacked me several times for no reason. When Murphy came into the dream, he stood by my side with his head down, asking for my forgiveness, and telling me he loved me, and that he never meant to hurt me. Of course I forgave him. He picked up his head and his tail wagged after I forgave him.

When I say they "talked" to me, it is hard to describe. They didn't talk in verbal words, but rather telepathic. It was communication without words, just one mind to another mind.

MICKEY PASKO-POWELL

Mark, Say Yes

Because of my failing health, I am wheelchair bound and rarely go out of the house. I was channel surfing the TV, and on the Oprah Winfrey Show, I heard about the spiritual book *Talking to Heaven* by James Van Praagh, the spiritual medium.

A week or so later I made a very rare excursion out of my home to go to the bookstore at the mall for a book on body language. The excursion was unique, also, in the fact that I rarely read books at the time. The last book I had read was over fifteen years ago. But I felt a need to go to the bookstore for some reason.

I didn't find a book on body language, but just as I was about to leave, my eye caught the light blue cover of the book *Talking to Heaven*, and I immediately grabbed a copy off the shelf and bought it. It was literally as though I felt an irresistible urge to read it. After I took it home I started to read it almost immediately, which was also surprising because I own lots of books that I haven't read. I was reading the first few chapters about how the people in the readings from the medium would sometimes get a message from loved ones from the spirit world. I began to reflect on my life and the people I would like to contact if I were given the chance.

I especially needed to reach a person named Mark who had passed, and to whom I had done a great wrong many years ago. I wanted to beg Mark for forgiveness. This great wrong affected my whole life and was one of the obstacles that caused me to despise myself. As I was reading the book, I summoned up the courage to address him personally and pleaded with him to forgive me. I asked him to leave me a sign if he forgave me, so I would know. Nothing happened, which didn't surprise me.

The next day I prayed to Jesus asking that Mark be allowed to leave me a message, but that I wouldn't take his lack of a response to mean he hadn't forgiven me; that it could mean that he just wasn't able to leave a message. Then again it could mean he hadn't forgiven me either. I began to think of what message I would recognize and claim. Immediately I said that I would recognize the name "Mark" with the word "yes" nearby (as in, yes, he forgives me). I prayed to Jesus asking that I would be able to recognize such a message as being from Mark, but that if he left me the message in some other way, or couldn't leave me the message at all, that it would be okay too.

Well, I began to look for "Mark" in everything I saw—on labels, boxes, in TV advertisements, etc. Nothing happened. No "Mark" anywhere. No surprise again. Although I read many people were helped, it was as if they were winners of some contest. The other guy always wins. I never do. I gave up trying to look, figuring if it happened, it happened.

I went back to finish reading *Talking to Heaven* and saw something that caused me to tremble and sob uncontrollably. As I was reading, the name "Mark" appeared on a page, with the word "yes" at the beginning of the very next sentence. The message that I had asked Mark to leave for me was written in the book I was reading! I couldn't believe it!

Suddenly, I felt a rush of love from Mark come into my body and felt my love returning to him. The pain that I had in my neck and shoulders, as if caused by a millstone, left me. This was a miracle that happened to me and I thanked Jesus for the joy and peace it has brought me. Not only did I know that Mark was safe on the other side, but I knew that he forgave me.

There is no doubt in my mind that the book was the instrument through which Mark's message reached me. I now understand why I suddenly bought and read the book, as though there had been someone guiding me. I realized that Jesus and Mark knew the prayer that I would say, long before I said it. They had influenced me, so that my prayed-for message would come through to give me peace.

LARRY

Grampy Came Back

My Grampy was eighty-seven when he passed. He had fallen a few months before his death and had to have hip surgery. We had a very old friend of the family help us out with him because the rest of us lived far away. In short, she robbed him blind! Wiped out his bank account and maxed out his credit cards.

Grampy found out about it and suffered a massive stroke. Never coming out of it and too tired to fight, in August 1995, he died. My guilt was awful. Why? She was *my* friend. I BEGGED Grampy to come to me. I BEGGED God. I needed to apologize to Grampy and beg for his forgiveness. I cried. I got angry. All sorts of emotions were running through me until that night. I fell asleep and the dream began.

In this dream my mom and I went to the front of the house that she and I grew up in, and where my Grampy lived for sixty-plus years. The front door was locked, so Mom said she would go around the back of the house to get in and for me to stay there. She left to go around to the rear of the house. Suddenly, the front door opened slowly. The first thing I saw in the house was Grampy's paintings; he was an artist.

I took a step in slowly when out from behind the door Grampy stepped into view. My heart started pounding and I was shaking so incredibly that I fell to the ground. I started crying and screaming, telling him how sorry I was over and over again.

Then he knelt down beside me (which at age eighty-seven he had been unable to do). He put his hand under my chin and lifted my head. He looked into my eyes and told me that it was NOT my fault. He said that he was fine; that he was happy, and he told me that he loved me. He told me he loved me, over and over, making sure that I truly understood how important I was to him. He said it was time for me to go on with my life and to try and forgive. We slowly stood up and grabbed onto each other and hugged so tightly that I can still feel it today.

When I awoke, I was sitting up in my bed with my arms out and crying. It was the most incredible feeling that I have ever felt in my entire life. I know that this was not just a dream. I was going through so much turmoil in my life. Grampy came to me, like he did in life, and made it all better. Even though I haven't had another "dream" like that at the time of this writing, I know he is with me every day.

DOROTHY HUREAU

My Reward for Forgiving

My story begins some thirty years ago, when I went to work as a truck driver for an appliance firm. Our foreman was very mean. Nobody liked him and he was on my back all the time. I guess the power of being a foreman went to his head. He died about five years ago, and I did not go to his funeral services.

About four months after he died, he would come to me in my dreams and I felt like he wanted my forgiveness. In the meantime, I had been reading books about God and what He said about love and forgiveness. Our Lord said to forgive seventy times seven. I became very spiritual thanks to these books.

Almost every night the foreman continued to come into my dreams; however, it was very hard to forgive someone who has treated you like you were nothing all of those years. But then I thought again about what the Lord said about forgiveness. So one night before going to sleep, I called the foreman's name and I told him, "I give you love and forgiveness."

About a week after I had given him love and forgiveness, I was laying on my bed watching a TV show on a Saturday afternoon. Suddenly I felt as if a hand had been placed on my shoulder. At the same time, out of the corner of my eye, I saw a light. I looked over toward the light and saw the face of my foreman as plain as day, and he was smiling at me. He looked very solid, even showing his teeth.

What I have learned from this after-death contact is this—if someone has given you a hard time in your life, forgive him or her anyway, for God will bless you if you do.

GEORGE STONE

* * *

AFTER-DEATH COMMUNICATIONS

CHAPTER 16

Godincidences

> I believe that the meaningful coincidences in our lives are really Godincidences—that is, God's divine providence and blessings entering into our lives at just the perfect time. I also believe our loved ones in spirit ask God for these blessings on our behalf too.

The Birthday Card From Both Coasts

Daddy passed in January 1999. My cousin had just been to Daddy's funeral and there my cousin told me, "Be sure to come to Oakland. Remember we are blood." This is because he grew up in another country, and we recently found each other here in America. Less than a month later, I would be traveling to San Francisco for my cousin's unexpected funeral.

With the loss of my father, and now the shock of my cousin's sudden passing, someone up in Heaven decided to give me a gift for my birthday, which was fast-approaching.

The thing about my dad was this: on my birthday, no matter where I lived, he would send me a card. But this year Daddy really knocked himself out on the one he sent me from Heaven. Here is my Godincidence: My son lived on the East Coast, and my daughter lived with me on the West Coast. My son's card was the first to arrive at my home, a few days earlier than my birthday. It was a white card with gold fancy print. It was not the usual cute, cheery, and colorful type he normally would send. No, this one was perfect since it was sent from a high spiritual source.

My daughter had not given me her card as yet, but showed up with one in her hand the day before my birthday. I opened the envelope, and when I looked at the front of the card, I felt disappointed. Disappointed because it appeared she merely had signed her name to her brother's card and had not even bought me one of her own. I said in a very sad, but annoyed tone, "Where did you get this card?" She replied, "At the pharmacy." "Really?" I said and opened the card up to see the inside.

It looked to be the same exact card that my son sent me—her signature was there—but my son's signature strangely was not. I couldn't believe this. I wondered how she was able to erase his signature from this card, which had been in ink! After all, this couldn't be! Besides he had written a paragraph to me in ink in his own handwriting, and where did that now disappear to?

My daughter insisted she bought me this card herself. So with doubt and skepticism I looked for my son's birthday card—not expecting to find a second one that was identical to my daughter's—but I did!

I knew that some very big event had just occurred. Both of my children, living on opposite coasts of the U.S., sent me the same identical card for my birthday. I was amazed.

I didn't know how such a miracle could have happened! I only knew that God had a hand in it. And absolutely Dad remembered my birthday. Oh yes he did, because I had been telling him, "Dad, this year I won't be getting a card from you when you always remembered my birthday no matter where I was living."

God is such an awesome God. He lets us know that His promise of eternal life is true, and our loved ones will and do touch our lives from the other side.

JENNY FLORES

Jimmy's Dialysis

I had lost a very dear friend Jimmy, who had been like a rock and a stabilizing force in my life at a time when I felt like I was drowning in quicksand. We had lost contact for a number of years, and I didn't find out that he had been called Home by God until after his funeral had already taken place.

Jimmy had been on dialysis, and I had never asked him many questions about it, but lately I wanted to know more. I had never been to a dialysis center, so it was all a mystery to me. It became an obsession of mine to find out more about Jimmy's dialysis, and I was wishing I knew someone else, also close to Jimmy, whom I could talk to about him.

Well, as "luck" would have it, I had an appointment with my massage therapist because I had I sprained my back "out of nowhere," after I just started training to run again. During the massage, my therapist asked me about my friend who died, because I had briefly mentioned him in the past. I said "Oh, Jimmy?" and I started to talk about Jimmy.

Then I told her how my toddler said his last name out of the blue. My toddler said, "There's my friend, Buster!" The massage therapist gasped! She said, "Jimmy Buster?" Well, I thought she couldn't possibly be talking about my Jimmy, but she was! She told me she had dated Jimmy. She said she used to be a dialysis nurse! Not only that, she was Jimmy's dialysis nurse! She worked for Jimmy's doctor and she and Jimmy had become very good friends.

So here I had the answer to my prayers. Not only did I have someone to talk to about Jimmy, who actually knew him, but someone who could tell me firsthand about Jimmy's dialysis! We both agreed there are no coincidences and she said, "Well hello, Jimmy Buster!" I told her Jimmy sent me to her. Thank you, God, for showing me that Jimmy is with me!

A few years prior to this discovery of our mutual Jimmy connection, this same massage therapist told me an amazing story. She told me that a male friend of hers called her one night. While on the phone, all the power in her house went out and she suddenly heard angelic children's voices singing. She looked, and her stereo was not on. No power! No lights! Nothing! It freaked her out and her male phone friend told her to look outside to see if the angelic music was coming from outside, while he waited on the phone.

She went outside, but there was no music out there. The music was definitely coming from inside her house! She became very upset and told her friend she had to go. Her friend thought all of this was very amusing, but before they hung up, a "window" appeared in the room, and she saw two men dressed in '40s attire. She screamed and they were gone. She hung up the phone and was very shaken by it all. I remembered this particular story vividly. After my massage therapist and I realized our mutual connection to Jimmy, she told me the man on the phone that night was Jimmy!

I recalled that way back when I first met Jimmy I had seen two angels near him, and I told him they looked to be male angels, and did he think I was crazy? He said, "No, it's not crazy, my brother and father passed away."

Incredible events. I will no longer say coincidences are just coincidences. And I am getting more of these happenings to prove it. I hope these stories may bring comfort to someone.

LAURI (TIGGER) PLESCO

My Dad Still Golfs With Me

My dad passed over in 2000. He was my best golf buddy. Through the years I have seen his presence on the golf course with me through hawks flying overhead, feeling invisible hands on my hips as I swung the golf club, and some miraculous golf shots!

In 2017, seventeen years after my dad passed, I lost a favorite magnetic golf ball marker while playing golf. It was originally a white colored one, but I had used orange magic marker to scribble on the top of it to differentiate it from a similar white one that my husband uses. I was disappointed because this was the second time I had lost one and they are about ten dollars to replace.

A month after losing my orange ball maker, my hubby and I were playing golf again. We came across a man who was playing by himself, so we asked him to join us. While playing, he pulled out a ball marker to place on the green. When I saw it, I was shocked! I recognized it as the marked-up orange magnetic one that I lost a month ago. I asked him where did it come from. He said he found it, but wasn't sure which golf course he found it on.

I asked him if he would trade me for a plastic one I had instead, and he said sure! I couldn't get over the Godincidence that we were playing golf with a complete stranger who just "happened" to have my orange marked-up ball marker!

However, this was more than a coincidence, for the very

next morning I was lying in bed and I was shown in my mind's eye that someone was giving me a gift. Then the next scene I was shown was a round token type of object, the size of the ball marker! So you see the return of my lost ball marker was a gift from Heaven—A Godincidence ADC. Thanks Dad!

CHRISTINE DUMINIAK

The Butterfly From Dad

Right before my parents died, I told my dad that I would be sad if I ever married and he wouldn't be at my wedding. His response to me was that he would always, where possible, be a butterfly on my shoulder.

As time went by, I eventually met a wonderful man and we decided to get married. As the date of the wedding drew near, I was greatly missing my beloved dad and my dear stepmum. I felt that every aspect of this wedding should have involved my dad being there with me, and it was emotionally very hard to plan it without him by my side.

A few days before the wedding, my friend Suzi phoned to let me know that she had been thinking about the "something borrowed, something blue" thing, and wanted to know if I would like to borrow something from her. She and her husband had lost their baby boy to non-Hodgkin's lymphoma. She was given a little pin after her baby died, and wanted to know if I would like to wear it. It turned out to be a little golden butterfly! I had goosebumps and many tears. This happened the day after I woke up crying, missing my dad so dreadfully much, and wishing hard for him to be at my wedding. This proved to me that he was, indeed, planning to be there with me!

MARIA

A Christmas Gift From Grandfather

My grandfather went Home to God on April 24, 2001. We were very close and I had been sad ever since, for I missed and loved him so.

I had been praying for some kind of contact from him. It was getting close to Christmas, December 22, 2001 to be exact. I was very down and dreading celebrating the first Christmas in twenty-five years without my dear grandfather. I knew it wouldn't be the same.

My husband surprised me and came home with someone's beloved pet cat that they had to give away. My husband just happened to be at the "right place at the right time" to adopt her. I loved her instantly!

Well, as Christmas Eve arrived, and as I sat all alone greatly missing my grandfather, I began listening to a few favorite songs. One of them happened to be "Wish You Were Here." Upon hearing this particular song, I started to cry. It had been eight months to the day my beloved grandfather went Home to God.

As I sat crying, my sweet new cat walked over to me and licked my hand, as if to say, "Don't be sad, everything will be all right." Suddenly the overwhelming sadness was gone and sweet happiness and blessed relief and comfort filled my heart instead. I now realized that my prayers had been answered.

This comforting companion was really a Christmas gift that my dear grandfather had arranged from Heaven to give to me. I also realized that my grandfather was aware of my sadness and loneliness, and he had prompted the cat to come to me and comfort me when I was at my lowest point. Because of this, my Christmas was simply wonderful.

RENEE

* * *

CHAPTER 17

Healings

All things are possible with the Great Physician.

Jesus and My Child

My daughter Deanna was two years old at the time. I was taking a shower and Deanna was lying on my bed. She was sick with an asthma-like illness. Because I had seen my brother battle asthma and almost die from it, I was very worried about her, so I gave my problem to the Lord, feeling that by His grace this would pass. Right after my prayer, I heard my daughter talking in my bedroom. I got out of the shower and asked her, "Who are you talking to?" She said, "Oh Jesus, Mommy. He said, 'Don't worry. He is going to take away my cough and make me all better.'" It has been two years since then. She has had some croup, but no asthma.

Deanna still sees Jesus. The last time she saw Him I was on the Internet and was part of a group that were praying for the healing of others in the Prayer Wave For After-Death Communication Chat Room. Deanna was sitting on my lap at the time and she said, "Look, Jesus is praying with us!"

DIANE

The Angel Gabriel

In 1995, my ten-year-old daughter Jennifer was diagnosed with a rare inoperable arteriovenous malformation of her brain. We were told that her chances of survival were zero percent. I begged our wonderful doctor to try and save her through an operation anyway. He said that he would operate, but her outcome would not be favorable. Even if she lived, she would probably lose her sight, hearing, and speech.

I prayed along with my family and friends to give my daughter strength and to ask the Lord to guide her doctor's hands and save my daughter's life.

After three procedures and the last surgery lasting almost twenty-seven hours, I knew that my prayers had been answered. My daughter had not only survived, but came out of these surgeries with only a slight impairment.

Even though throughout the months preceding her surgeries my daughter was in terrible pain, she seemed to have a sense of calmness about her. I learned why when we came home from the hospital after the third operation.

While sitting in our living room at home, my daughter Jen asked me if it were possible to see her guardian angel. I asked her why? She said that her angel was with her throughout the preceding months she had been awaiting her surgeries in three different hospitals. She told me that, whenever she was scared or in pain, she would just look to her right and she would see, as she described it, the brightest night light she ever saw.

She said the angel would raise what almost looked like a hand and wave to her. When the angel did this, she would no longer be afraid. I asked her if her angel was still with her even now at home. Very seriously she said, "Yes." Not that I had doubts that she saw a bright light, but I thought perhaps the visual phenomena she was experiencing may have been as a result of her surgery. I turned out all the lights in the room to make it completely dark. I asked her again what she saw. Jen said, very peacefully, "Yes, there is my angel waving to me. I can see my angel. It is the brightest light I ever saw."

I knew then that God had let my daughter see her angel to give her the strength to survive her ordeal, while He was healing her through the surgeon's hands.

After a few weeks I found my daughter crying. I asked her why. She said, "My angel went away." I told her that her angel is always with her, and she would just not need to see her in that way anymore because she was now going to live and be okay.

About a year later I went to a renowned medium for a reading. Before she began talking about me (and I had not told her anything about my daughter or what she had been through), the medium told me that she could see that I have a very special daughter. What she told me was profound. She said she could see that my daughter had been through brain surgery and that she, in reality, should not have survived. She told me that God sent the Angel Gabriel to be with Jen to give her comfort and to be with the doctor to guide his hands throughout the surgery. It was because of our faith in God that my daughter is alive and well. It is further proof that our faith and prayers can indeed work miracles, if it is God's Will for us.

MARY ANN & JENNIFER SEABOLD

Jesus Heals A Muslim

I would like to share with you a mystical experience that happened in my home. I had a young crippled woman, who was a homeless refugee, staying with me who hardly spoke any

English. Her name is Anni. She is a Muslim and her religion does not really teach her about Jesus Christ.

We had a nurse come in to do physical therapy on Anni's crippled legs. One day the nurse knelt at Anni's bedside and prayed. We couldn't budge Anni during those prayers, and she seemed to be in a trance. At first I got a little scared. I then called her and said her first and last name and added, "In the name of Jesus Christ get up!" On the second calling she woke up. After she awoke, Anni explained to us what was actually happening to her as she lay in a trance.

She said during these healing prayers, she was surrounded by this man wearing the robes she sees on my Sacred Heart candle. The man on my candle is Jesus Christ. She said Jesus had been talking to her while she lay in a trance.

She also said that, while the nurse was on her knees praying, there were angels with her surrounding the bed. The angels, too, were on their knees. One angel had her hands raised to the heavens. Another angel had her hands crossed over her chest. Another was healing with the nurse over Anni, while another angel was pushing her hands into Anni's stomach, and taking what ailed her stomach and pulling it out. Anni said that when the angel pulled it out, the sound it made was a loud pop; she had felt the knot in her stomach suddenly release, and her stomach felt hot.

When the nurse raised her hand over my refugee friend, Anni said that the nurse's hands gave out lots of yellow light. There were other angels around, too, and they were smiling and all were praising God. Then this Being spoke—the man in those long robes. At this point she could not see His face because there were many different colored lights around His face. The rays of light roamed about in a circular fashion. She said Jesus spoke to her. He said, "Why are you sad? Don't be sad. Anything your heart needs I will give to you. You are not alone. I am with you all the time. You will soon get everything you need. Don't be afraid. This is my daughter (the healing nurse). My daughter will help you, and I will help her."

Then Anni said she saw me walking with two female angels by my side, and she saw my brain-injured husband, who was recuperating and relearning how to walk, with a male angel. My friend said, "Jenny, when your nurse leaves this house, you don't have to be afraid because you have no strength. You have other angels doing the work for you. You're afraid your husband will fall, but they are holding him up for you."

I was amazed. I also watched Anni's legs while the nurse did a second healing that totally separated her atrophied legs. Well, after this experience, Anni kept saying, "Thank you, Jesus." I told her, "Jesus is real. He was here on earth and He made many miracles. He is still making miracles." Although Anni is still in a wheel chair, her legs were separated from being locked together, and her stomach ailment was healed that day.

JENNY FLORES

Death was Imminent

I had been a born-again Christian since 1975. God has healed me several times. A few of these were miracles, but then that is nothing new for Him as far as I am concerned.

In 1986, I moved to Florida from Georgia. While living in Florida, I caught double pneumonia and it was very serious. I went to see a doctor who gave me medicine and wanted to immediately put me in the hospital. I had no insurance at the time, so I felt I could not afford to go. After four weeks I was no better, in fact, I was much, much worse and could hardly take a shallow breath. One night during this illness, I was all alone upstairs in my bedroom, propped up on three pillows, struggling hard to breathe. I was lying on my waterbed. It was motionless because I did not even have enough strength to move, let alone breathe. I knew I was not long for this world. I prayed, "Father God, please do not take me Home yet, who will take care of my babies?"

All of a sudden, I heard four footsteps walk from my room's balcony area to my bed. I should have been scared, but instead I felt extremely peaceful.

The mattress of my waterbed started to move and roll gently as I watched one of God's holy angels lay down beside me. I was astounded that an angel would have any weight at all and could actually make my waterbed move.

I next saw the very peaceful presence of Jesus standing at the foot of my bed. My entire room began to fill with a comforting warmth and a cloud-like substance. That was when I knew my Father God was there with me.

Suddenly it did not matter what happened on this earth. I now desired to go on Home. Talk about being in the Lord's Presence! At that moment, I cared no more for earthly things; in fact, I had absolutely no cares at all. All I wanted was to be with my God. That was my last thought as I fell off to sleep.

The next morning when I awoke, I was one hundred percent well. No cough, no weakness, no breathing problems. It was as if I had never been sick at all!

I learned something during this miraculous visit. Yes, I love my family and I wanted to see my children grow up, but when we are in His Presence nothing else matters to us. I have never in my life felt such total peace and freedom, and I have never felt the unconditional love I felt that night.

I realized that earth is not my home. Just a stopping place to learn, grow spiritually, and to minister to others. I got to hear an angel of the Lord come into my room and cover me that night to protect and heal me. I got to feel such an overwhelming presence of my Father in Heaven, nothing else mattered but going to Him. From that day forward my faith has never wavered.

Even after all these years, it is still as clear in my mind as if it had happened yesterday. What a wonderful God we have.

Love to all in His Name.

DONNA BOWMAN

Kendall's Miracle

As my husband Kendall lay near death from a brain injury due to a fall on October 5, 2001, and the doctors said he wouldn't make it, I came to my Prayer Wave for After-Death Communication family and posted on the message board for prayers for a miracle. All of the prayers brought great power, and we received a miracle around Christmas time of 2001 because Kendall suddenly started breathing on his own.

I also wished and actually dreamt that we were on a cruise to celebrate his recovery. Eventually that wish did come true. We did get to take that cruise the following October 6, 2002– one year and one day after his injury.

When we boarded the ship, Kendall was in a wheel chair, still on a feeding tube, and wearing Depends' diapers. Kendall could not walk steadily, was not able to swallow, and not able to use the toilet on his own. I had no help in taking care of Kendall during this dream-come-true vacation, but I trusted that God was always with us and even helping us on this cruise.

The first day of the cruise we were sitting in the dining room, and I wanted Kendall to feel as if he were part of the cruise. So for show only, I gathered a plate of food from the buffet for Kendall and placed it before him on our table. I assumed he would be too full from his tube feeding to even want to eat, and that he would ignore the food, as usual. To my horror and terror he began to eat his mashed potatoes! I expected disaster to befall him! I was so afraid that he would start choking or be harmed in some way before I had a chance to pull the food away.

God must have sent His angels because all went perfectly well. Kendall didn't choke, and was actually able to swallow! Kendall further astonished me when he next said, "You know who was just here? Marge. She was just gabbing away like she always does. You're gonna be okay."

Marge is Kendall's first wife, who passed over many years before. But Marge's spirit was able to relay to Kendall that I was going to be okay and that I had nothing to fear when it came to my husband's well-being. I have never spoken to Kendall about my fears concerning his welfare, so I knew this information was something he was not aware of.

The third day of the cruise was the hardest day since we boarded. All morning long I had pushed him around in the wheel chair and I was dead tired. In the afternoon we returned to our room. I was so sleepy, yet, I would not allow myself to fall asleep, for fear that Kendall would go off alone in his wheel chair and, perhaps, fall into the sea.

I started telling God my troubles, and after talking to God, Kendall suddenly fell off to sleep. Even though I was relieved that he did, I was still telling God my woes. I said, "Oh God, I wish there was someone I could call to help us. They don't do people-sitting on board this ship, I bet."

AFTER-DEATH COMMUNICATIONS

I started drifting in and out of sleep myself while Kendall slept. Finally, I must have dozed off heavily. The telephone suddenly rang. The caller urgently asked in an alarming tone of voice, "Do you need help?" I was groggy but suspicious about who could possibly have known that I needed help. I knew no one on the cruise and we kept pretty much to ourselves.

Being cautious about who the unknown caller was, I had the presence of mind to simply say, "Well, thanks to God, I don't need help. Why? Who are you?" The man on the phone had a foreign accent and urgently repeated, "Do you need help? I just got a call that you needed help."

I said to the man on the phone, "What was the call that you received that told you I needed help?"

He answered, "I just got a call from your room saying you needed help."

I said back to the caller, "How could this be possible, since we were both asleep. Do you have caller ID?" He said, "Yes, it says Room 2002." This was our room number. I said, "Thank you very much, but I never called you, and thanks to God, I don't need help."

He said he was from the Purser's Office, so I immediately headed right down there to find out who called the Purser's Office. Upon further questioning, the crew member said he only received a telephone call in which a voice said, "I need help!" and the caller hung up. So he hit something comparable to *69. He looked at the caller ID and it was our room number that showed up.

I suddenly realized this was an after-death communication message—thanks to God. God heard my prayer for help. He was telling me to have no fear and no desperation; that on this cruise we would receive help; that even though I felt alone, I was not. I really felt like God was talking to me through this unexplained phone call offering me help, and I was amazed at the thought of His Presence finding me in this tiny spot on earth.

But the heavenly help did not stop there. More miracles started happening. Suddenly and to my astonishment, Kendall was eating mashed potatoes with gravy and desserts all during the whole cruise! Not only that, Kendall started to walk with a steady gait and no longer needed the wheel chair! As if these miracles weren't enough, Kendall even abandoned the diapers. He did not even need one diaper for he was now going to the bathroom on his own, and I hadn't bladder trained him at all! He just stopped using diapers and started going by himself. Kendall miraculously did all these things during our cruise to celebrate the miracle of life he received.

You see this Prayer Wave For After-Death Communication group prayed with me for a miracle and God showed and revealed His face to me and to the people at Prayer Wave. God bless you.

JENNY FLORES

* * *

CHAPTER 18

Help

Help from the Lord comes in endless ways. Sometimes it is through His using a loved one in spirit to answer our prayers. Sometimes it is through God's revealing His plan to us.

The Toilet ADC

I was devastated when my dear brother Jimmy passed. We were very close and I could always rely on him to help me, especially so when I became a single mom with four young children to raise on my own.

One day I could have really used my brother Jimmy's help and strength, after my four-year-old filled the toilet with a hair spray bottle, bottle tops, make-up brushes, toothbrush covers, and hair bows. Oh, let's not forget the Q-tips! I didn't know he had flushed the toilet before I even got there! This completely stopped up the toilet big time!

After a disgusting time of fishing it all out, I tried everything to unclog it including Liquid Plumber, Drano, a wire hanger, and plunging it to death, but nothing worked. I had no money to call a plumber, so we had a mess here as you can well imagine.

I waited awhile and decided to try plunging it again but no luck. I plunged that toilet for four hours as hard as I could . . . NOTHING! I was so tired and disgusted. So finally with my arms about to break, I stepped back and said out loud, "Lord, pleeeeease help me. I can't fix this thing and I can't pay someone. Please help me or, Jimmy, come down here and stand behind me and help me. I am not strong enough."

Well, guess what happened next? The toilet flushed! It just flushed on its own, and I did not even touch it. I looked at it with the plunger in my hand and said, "Oh . . . oh . . . oh . . . oh . . is it fixed?" I looked to my side and saw my brother Jimmy standing there! He was wearing jeans, a buttoned-up shirt, and a baseball style cap, like he always wore. He looked transparent and shimmery, yet he was in good focus. He was smiling and then poof he was gone!

I burst out crying and my kids heard me and came running in yelling, "What? What?" I just fell to the floor crying and told them what had just happened. My young son nonchalantly said, "Well, Mom, he's always here. He helps me all the time." My young daughter said she sees him as clear as day at times too. I have never had this sort of thing happen to me before; I was amazed!

I went back and tried flushing the toilet over and over, just to be sure it really was working, and it was definitely fixed. It worked every time.

I thanked Jimmy and God a million times. My brother was truly there. I saw him and I wasn't scared at all. I called my momma and told her and she said, "Oh, I wish I was there. He fixed it for you." I said, "I know, Momma, he was here for real."

I miss him so much. If I ever had any type of doubt that he was with me helping me, this was the proof I needed to show there are no coincidences! I asked for help to fix the toilet and I got it! Thank You, Jimmy, for helping your little sister again in her time of trouble. I love you, Big Brother!

CANDI

Heaven's Clue

My dog Pudden was stolen. This was at a time when I was so grief-stricken over the death of my close friend Jimmy. I thought that Pudden was probably better off with another owner, anyway, because I had nothing left emotionally to give. Three months later, I really wanted my dog back, so one night I sat down before going to bed and prayed to God to let Pudden come back to me. I instinctively knew she was still alive and someone else was taking care of her. I told God I was healing now and was ready to take better care of Pudden and to be a more attentive dog owner.

That very night after my prayer, I dreamt Pudden was running home to me down a street named Clarendon. Since I have gotten many validating dreams in the past, I hoped that this dream was a message from Heaven for me.

I am a runner, and two days after my prayer and dream, I went for a long run. When I returned from my run, Pudden was back home! She had a tag on. Her new owner had renamed her and this owner lived on Clarendon!

I feel so blessed that God gives me these dream messages from Heaven. And I now know that we are spiritually contacted through our dreams. I hope my experience may comfort someone else too.

LAURI PLESCO (TIGGER)

AFTER-DEATH COMMUNICATIONS

The Casino Hits

My friend Ruby's mother had passed eleven years earlier. As life can be sometimes, her husband lost his job. One day she sat down in her living room feeling extremely sad and desperate. She began to speak to her mother in prayer. "Mommy, what am I going to do? My husband has lost his job. Mommy, please help me. What are we going to do?"

One night shortly thereafter Ruby exhausted went to bed early. As Ruby lay sleeping, her mother entered her dreams. "Get up, Ruby. I'm going to help you. I want you to get up and go to the Indian Casino tonight. There you will win a jackpot."

In her dream Ruby was reluctant. She didn't have the money to spend on gambling. She didn't want to do it, so she said, "Awww, Mommy, nooooo."

But her mother was persistent. "Ruby, I want you to get up now. Hurry up. Go now." She even showed her the board lit up with numbers to play.

Ruby woke up still feeling reluctant to go to the casino. She did not even recall the numbers shown to her. She took fifty dollars with her and arrived at the casino at 9 p.m.

At 1 a.m. in the morning Ruby hit her first jackpot. It was nineteen thousand dollars!

During the course of one year Ruby made eighty-one thousand dollars in jackpot hits. I was there with her when she placed five dollars into the video slot machine and won twenty-five thousand dollars.

Lately, those wins have subsided. But what a message of help from an angel!

JENNY FLORES

Grandma's Passing—Not Till October

In February 1997, I woke up and told my husband that we needed to go to Michigan in October because that's when my grandma was going to die. He looked at me sort of weird and said, "OK." I kept a mental note of that October date.

In June of that year my dad called and said my grandma had deteriorated, was in the hospital, and the doctors were saying she would not make it through the night. He wanted me to come up for the funeral. After the phone call I went and meditated, and I got the message that she would not die, but instead she would get better and go back into the nursing home. I called my dad back and told him my message and that I would be up in October to see my grandma. He was not happy about this at all. I wrote my dad a letter so he would understand. I told him that I would be up in October and hoped that what I was telling him would give him some comfort.

Well, you guessed it . . . grandma got better, to everyone's amazement, and went back into the nursing home! She was not eating in the nursing home though and my cousin, a doctor, tried to persuade her by asking if she knew what would happen if she didn't eat. She said "Yes." He asked her what that would be, and she said, "I'll fly away," with a laugh. I believe she knew.

In October my husband and I flew to Michigan. I decided to run my first marathon there in Detroit and then visit my grandma. My friend Amy asked if I thought my grandma would die when I came up and I said, "I'm packing a dress for the funeral." She gasped! But I told her it was okay.

I ran my marathon and it was a beautiful, magical day. I felt a presence with me the whole way. The next day I sighed and told my husband it was time to go see my grandma. We drove over there and I went alone into her room. I was afraid Grandma would not recognize me, so I brought a picture with me of when I was three years old in which I was standing beside my grandma.

She was sleeping when I went into the room, so I sat down and looked through her picture albums. I suddenly looked up and she was looking at me. I walked over to her, showed her the picture and told her, "Hi. It's Lauri, your granddaughter, the little girl in the picture coming all the way from Georgia to see you." She looked at the picture and a tear ran down her face. She then looked at me and closed her eyes for good.

My dad and aunt appreciated hearing this and also told me that they had never seen their mother shed a tear.

LAURI (TIGGER) PLESCO

The Jackpots Were a Gift From God

At one point in my life I owned an apartment and I was renting it to a woman who became mentally ill. Not only did she not pay her rent for three months, but she also destroyed the apartment. I was worried about how I was going to pay for all of the repairs. I did not have enough money to cover all the damages caused by this tenant.

While I had this huge financial burden on my shoulders, I decided to go to the casino for a day of fun to try and get my mind off of my troubles. I am not a big gambler, so I was playing the slot machines. All of a sudden I felt the Blessed Mother's veil cover me. This is an experience I have felt many times before in my life. The next thing I knew, I hit the jackpot! I couldn't believe it.

I hit the jackpot, not once, but three times that night! The woman attendant at the casino said she has never seen anything like my jackpot winnings the whole time she worked there! Over the next three-week period, I would receive a certain sign, which was a vision of the Infant of Prague (Baby Jesus), to play a certain slot machine. I followed that heavenly guidance and I hit the jackpot at least two more times. My winnings totaled about eleven thousand dollars over that three-week period of time.

This money was a gift from God to cover all the mounting bills that were heaped upon me due to the tenant problem I had. I smiled and said, "Thank you, God, for all of this."

LINDA MARIE

Note from Christine Duminiak : Although Linda would never mention this, I know she constantly helps her church financially, as well as other people in need. God must be rewarding her for her acts of kindness and compassion.

* * *

AFTER-DEATH COMMUNICATIONS

* * *

CHAPTER 19

Lost & Found

> At times God sends our loved ones to help us "retrieve" missing items. These items may even disappear and reappear mysteriously and with no logical explanation, yet we know we had spiritual help and are being watched over.

Dragonfly Earrings

Dragonflies seem to be the latest marvelous sign from our son John's spirit, and a very dear friend of mine had given me a pair of beautiful dragonfly earrings. The earrings just touched my heart because they reminded me of John and all those dragonfly signs he has been sending.

When I received the earrings, I put them on and never took them off. Well, one morning, I got up for work and went into the bathroom to put on my make-up. It was then that I noticed that one of the earrings had come out during the night. I walked over to my bed, which is near my dresser, and I took the remaining earring off and laid it safely and carefully next to the clock on my dresser. I didn't want to lose that one as well.

I began to hunt for the lost earring, as it meant so very much to me, not only because it was a gift, but because it represented a sign from my son. I took off the blankets, searched the bed, got down on my knees, and felt under the bed. I looked in the hallway, the laundry room, and the bathrooms but still could not find it. I knew I had to leave for work soon, so I thought I would look for it again when I got back home from work.

I finished my make-up and sat back down on the bed to finish getting dressed. Well, my eye caught sight of an amazing sight. Sitting six inches from the one dragonfly earring I had taken off earlier this morning was its match—the lost earring! Both earrings were now sitting together next to the clock! The biggest relief and smile came over my face. My baby was watching his mom, knew of my distress, found the missing earring, and placed it where I would find it. God bless that son of mine.

CATHYJMF, & KEVIN MURTAUGH

The Missing Angel Story

About seven years ago I had a near-drowning experience, and three years ago I posted my experience on a Website for angel stories. Ever since that time, I had been unable to relocate the Website and the story I posted there. I thought I checked every angel site under the title "Angel Stories" and tried every other way to find it. Also my computer had crashed after I posted the story, which meant the story was no longer saved in my computer's files. Therefore, I was unable to retrieve it that way either.

Well, recently I was looking for something totally unrelated, and a strong urge came over me to ask my dearest friend Barb, who had passed recently, to help me find the story. I did not question this feeling, or think it silly because of all of the spiritual signs I had been getting from her recently.

So, I asked Barb to help me find the story I wrote. Within ten minutes I was led to a Website where angel stories were listed. I searched under the title of "Inspiration" and there was my story, entitled "Father's Day." I was so totally overwhelmed by the help I had just received.

I felt like Barb was right there beside me finding that story for me. This is truly an awesome and incredible happening for me after a three-year search. Of course I thanked God for allowing Barb to communicate with me this way and in so many other ways!

I now pray daily for signs from my beloved friend Barb. Sometimes I ask for specific signs, such as a rose, a dove to appear, or angels because Barb always said I was like her angel. I have asked for music ADCs and always receive these upon request. Often, I receive these ADCs without first asking. I know she knows what I need and the best ways to contact me.

KIM S. MANGAN

Blind As A Bat

At home I have two pairs of reading glasses, one of which is my favorite pair. One evening in the beginning of November, only four and a half months after my love Honey passed over, I was on our front porch talking on the phone to my nephew in Dallas. I was preparing to fly there soon. All of my nieces, their husbands and children were going to be meeting there to celebrate Thanksgiving a week earlier than the holiday. My sister (only sibling) was dying of lung cancer, and the hospice staff felt that she might not last until the actual holiday.

Anyway, I had been talking to my nephew and reading the airline schedule. I came back into the house and laid my glasses down. Not two minutes later I went to put the glasses back on and I could not find them! I get so infuriated with myself when things like that happen. I could have something in my hand one minute and not have a clue as to where it is the next! They say it's age . . . . Well, I looked high and low for those glasses. I retraced my steps inside of the house and even looked in other areas I knew I didn't go. No glasses! I said, "Honey, please help me find my glasses! You know I can't read without them." But still, no glasses.

The next evening after work I was in the kitchen when I heard something fall in the living room. I went in to look and saw a book had fallen out of the bookcase! It wasn't teetering on the edge; I hadn't just put the book there. It had been there for a while in the bookcase. When I bent down to pick it up, I turned my head and there, on the floor by the couch, were my glasses! I thanked Honey for finding them for me.

JO LYNN

The Joke Is On Me

In February 2000, my beloved daddy Stanley crossed over to God. Three months later it was Mother's Day and my sweet, thoughtful husband gave me a lovely gold chain with a gold heart pendant attached. The heart was the size of a quarter and had engraved on it the words, "I love you." I cherished this necklace and the sentiment behind it. Every night I would religiously take it off and carefully put it in a specific cleared-off spot on my bureau, so I wouldn't misplace it.

One morning I got up, took a shower, and went to put on my necklace, but the necklace was GONE! I was very upset and looked all over the bureau for it. I must have searched for about five minutes. I couldn't understand how it could be missing because of my faithful ritual of putting it in that specific area of my bureau every time I took it off. Finally, I went out into the family room where my husband was, and I asked him if he had seen it or moved it. He said, "No," and seemed a bit annoyed that I may have lost it.

I walked back into our bedroom and proceeded to look all over the bureau again. It was still missing. I then decided to get down on my hands and knees and search the carpet. I immediately found the gold chain on the rug–but no heart pendant, just the chain. I got up off the floor and glanced at the bureau again. On the bureau in the very spot where I had placed the pendant the night before, the pendant had suddenly reappeared! Yet, only a few seconds before, it was still missing! And there had been no one physically in the room, but me! When I told my husband about the mysterious reappearance of the pendant and wondered out loud if my dad's spirit had something to do with it, my husband said, "Oh you must have accidentally pushed it out from under some things when you were looking around." Yet, even though I knew his explanation did not jive with the facts, I began to doubt myself and the fact that it might be an ADC from my dad.

A few nights later I was given the real explanation for the mysterious disappearance and reappearance of my necklace. I had a dream in which my dad's spirit came and visited me. During this dream, he showed me that he was the one who was responsible for the mischief surrounding my necklace.

When I woke up from that dream message, I realized that my dad was having fun with me the other day, when he temporarily hid the necklace and pendant from me. He was "showing off a bit" with his new found supernatural powers in his spiritual body. And boy did I delight in this knowledge and this cute prank pulled off by my precious dad. "You Go, Daddy-O!" Thank You, Lord, for allowing these wonderful visits.

CHRISTINE DUMINIAK

Bryan Came Through For Me

One evening, after I took off a pair of blue lapis lazuli earrings, I carefully put the backs on each one of them securely. I was in the act of putting these earrings into a jewelry box on top of my dresser when one fell out of my hand. I made sure to keep my eyes on it as it fell, so I would not miss where it would land. Just before it hit the floor the earring disappeared. I noticed at the same instant it disappeared, that right next to my right knee, there was a moving swirl with a slight grayish haze, and I thought, "No, that can't be . . ." I searched under the dresser, lifting the suitcase lying there, sure the earring had to land just under or close to the edge of the dresser. There was NO earring there.

I remembered that earlier I had asked Bryan (my love who is now in spirit) to show me some tangible physical proof of his spiritual presence by moving something in my room. Earlier that day I had been working on a book about Bryan and had been feeling his presence and receiving telepathic communication, yet I still had doubts if Bryan was really there communicating with me (and I wasn't just crazy). I felt that Bryan could remove my doubts about his presence if he were to physically move something for me.

So after the earring vanished, I said out loud, "Okay, in the morning I will find my earring on the floor." I was half-expecting, half-doubting that Bryan would find the earring and put it in a place where I would easily see it and that he would honor my request to show me physical proof of his presence.

The next day I had completely forgotten about the lost earring until I went into my jewelry box to retrieve the blue lapis earrings. There was only one earring there, and as I frantically tried to remember where I'd last seen them both, I suddenly realized that my left hand now held the missing earring! Not only was my left hand suddenly holding my missing earring, but my right held the earring back that was on the earring post the night before when it fell! Which meant that not only did "someone" retrieve the fallen missing earring and had put it into my hand just then, but that "someone" also took the back off of the earring, too, and placed it in my other hand!

It was so amazing that this could actually be done, and there was no doubt in my mind that this event actually occurred.

Since this happened, all doubt of Bryan's spiritual presence being truly with me has been removed from my mind.

ROBIN

* * *

AFTER-DEATH COMMUNICATIONS

*   *   *

CHAPTER 20

Unexplained Objects

Our loved ones seem to find some of the most intriguing ways to communicate with us. No matter how insignificant the object is, if you feel like it was meant especially for you, then claim that as an ADC; our loved ones will combine ADCs with thoughts that this was caused by their spiritual hand.

Potpourri vs. Law of Gravity

My mother lived with my husband and me for many years before her passing, which was eleven years ago. My husband was a yeller and there were many times when my mother wanted to give him a piece of her mind, but never did. If you knew my mom you would understand that she was the sweetest person on this earth and cherished the time she was given to spend with my family, including my husband too. When my mother passed I prayed to God for her, and I prayed to her.

A few weeks after her passing, my husband was in our family room in front of the fireplace placing more wood on the fire and "yelling" at me once again. Only this time in the middle of his yelling, he was stopped dead in his tracks by a basket of potpourri that was hurled towards him. The basket had been sitting on a shelf about three feet off to the side from where he was kneeling. To reach my husband from that far away, the basket had to have been thrown over to where he was by someone. For the basket to have fallen down on its own, and to adhere to the laws of gravity, it would have simply fallen straight down—not hurled outwards that far away.

I was blamed for that basket of potpourri being flung at my husband, the only thing was, I was in the kitchen and nowhere near that area of the family room!

I love you, Mom.

COLLEEN

My Dad's Coffee

It was April 1, the anniversary of my dad's returning Home to God. My husband Mark had risen early that morning to get ready for work. He likes his coffee just like my dad did when Dad was still with us here on earth. My husband had only met my dad once, so he wasn't familiar with his style or his sense of fun.

Mark spilled a little bit of coffee, got a sponge, cleaned it up, turned to the sink to rinse the sponge out, and felt a rush of cold air. When he turned back, his coffee cup was half empty and there was coffee spilled on the counter again! He rebuked the spirit, but the spirit didn't leave. Dad just wanted a little coffee!

I felt my dad's presence all day after that. The candle I lit burned bright and tall and danced wildly whenever we talked about Dad.

My sister-in-law also had a coffee ADC from my dad on that very same day, April 1. She had risen early before anyone else. She doesn't put sugar in her coffee, but when she left the room to get her glasses and returned to drink her coffee, there was sugar in it. She felt Dad's presence and heard him chuckle!

BJ

Jesus First

First, let me say that Honey and I were of different religions. I'm Jewish and Honey was Protestant. Religion was not the sole differences for us. We were on opposite ends of everything. Pick a category—politics, money, taste in furniture, clothing, etc., etc. We didn't agree, but we loved each other more than words can describe. I miss him with all my heart, now that he has passed.

Six months had gone by since he passed. On this particular morning, after I finished getting dressed for work, I was coming down the stairs when I stepped on a hard lump that was right in the middle of a step. I looked to see what it was and found a lapel pin with the words "Jesus First." I had never seen this pin before, but then Honey could have put it away someplace. However, since Honey passed, there wasn't anyone living in the house aside from me. And certainly it would have taken me less than six months to see this pin on the stairway if it had been there before, but there it was, plainer than day.

I sat on the step and sobbed. I knew it was a "Hello" from Honey.

JO LYNN

The Swinging Cups

A few years back, my son Jimmy went to New York on a business trip and brought me a hand-blown glass punch bowl set with cups hanging from the sides. The ladle is beautifully trimmed in gold. I put it in my china hutch for all to see and I loved it dearly. My hutch is across from my kitchen table.

After my son passed away in January 2001, I was sitting at my table crying because I missed him so, when all of a sudden something told me to look at the punch bowl set. As I looked at it, I was amazed to say the least! All the cups were swinging really fast from side to side and almost turning over upside down, as if imitating a pouring motion.

Thinking no one would believe this, I called my nephew to come over to my house and see for himself. And I said to my son's spirit, "Jimmy, please don't stop doing this. Please let someone else besides me see you do this."

When my nephew came into the kitchen area and saw this happening, he was just as amazed as I was. A few minutes later my daughter Candi came over to visit. I excitedly told her about it, and she went to look for herself. When Candi looked at the cups, they were still swinging.

My daughter stood there for hours talking to the cups to see what they would do. We even told it to stop. We said, "If this is you, Jimmy, make it stop." The cups would go from shaking wildly to a complete standstill! We told other family members about this too, and as they came over to talk to the cups, the cups would again start swinging for their benefit.

Since Jimmy passed, you can be sitting at the table and thinking of him and sometimes the cups will start swinging. At other times, if you go up to the cups and ask Jimmy to show us if he's there, they will start swinging too. At times, they will actually turn completely upside down and still not fall off of the punch bowl where they are hanging from!

I know my son is with me! I love him so much.

THELMA MILAM

Wind Chimes

Before my sister Lee passed away from a lengthy and courageous battle with cancer, we had many opportunities to talk about our afterlife beliefs. She told me to remember her whenever I heard wind chimes.

Well the neatest thing happened three weeks after her passing. We were in the process of moving to a new house, and I was in the house thinking of Lee and wishing that she was there with me to share in this newest event in my life. After that wish, I heard wind chimes! My mother-in-law was walking into the room holding my wind chimes. She told me that the strangest thing had just happened. She came across the chimes in a box and took them out extremely carefully and slowly, so they wouldn't bang against each other. When they should have stopped making any slight sounds at all, they continued to move and chime, as if some unseen force were pushing them back and forth repeatedly. And they wouldn't stop doing this! It continued on for such a long period of time, unnaturally so, that we knew the wind chimes were being moved by someone—my sister Lee.

Needless to say, I now have wind chimes hanging up inside my new house hoping for more communication from my sweet sister Lee.

COLLEEN

S For Stella

I went to the cemetery where my mom and dad are buried. I know that neither of them "hang out" at the cemetery; they are always with me. However, I had a Christmas tree with me to place on their grave. They share one grave, as they both wished to be cremated.

Anyway, I got to "talking with Mom" complaining about how poorly the cemetery is being taken care of and about the grass on the grave. This was the same thing my mom would complain and be irritated about when she and I would go to "visit" Dad.

I was picking up stones and debris from the grave, when I picked up this small object and wondered what the heck it was? After I turned it over to get a better look at it, I realized it was the letter "S" made out of plastic. My mom's name begins with an "S." Her name is Stella.

After finding this S, I felt this was a gift and a hello from Mom, to let me know she is with me for sure.

MICKEY PASKO-POWELL

The Unread Letter

A year before my brother passed over, he had been burned badly in a brush fire in his yard when a gas can exploded. He was in critical condition for months. We are a very close family, but unfortunately, his wife hated the rest of his family from the very beginning. So when my brother was in the hospital his wife tried, unsuccessfully, to stop all of us from visiting him. I would drive the three hours it took to visit him anyway.

One day in January, I decided to write my brother a letter explaining how his wife tried to keep us from seeing him and told him that she did not succeed in her quest! I told him how scared we were about his accident, and that we loved him so much. I told him about all of the prayers that were being said for him, and that I'd be here for him, no matter what!

I planned on giving the letter to him at a later date. I put the letter in my dresser drawer, under my summer clothes for the time being, but I never did give him that letter after all.

A year went by and, sadly, it was now the day of my brother's memorial service. I came home to try and deal with my intense grief. As I walked into my bedroom, I saw the letter inexplicably lying on my bedroom floor, and the letter had been opened. Yet no one had been to my home in days!

Before that day I had wondered why I had never given him that letter before, though I wished I had. I wanted him to know how his wife had treated us and how badly it hurt. But my brother must have known my thoughts this day—the day of his memorial service. He must have known that I would be feeling lost and regretting his never having read that letter, so he came and read it for my benefit. By placing the now opened letter on my bedroom floor, he showed me he finally knew and understood what had gone on while he was in the hospital and about my hurt feelings, and it made me feel better.

I just looked around the room and said, "Thanks, Jimmy."

CANDI

* * *

AFTER-DEATH COMMUNICATIONS

* * *

CHAPTER 21

Out of Body Experiences

Out of body experiences are when our spirits spontaneously leave our physical bodies for a brief period of time. When God allows this mystical experience to occur, there is usually a very tranquil and peaceful state of being that accompanies it. Perhaps it is similar to what we feel when we first cross over.

God Embraced Me

My first out of body experience, OBE, happened when I was dating my husband. I had asked my mother to wake me up at a certain time. When the time approached, she tried to wake me for an hour but was unable to. This was because my spirit was out of my physical body. At first I saw a bright light that consumed by body. It felt great. I was warm all over and then I started to rise, away from my physical body. Since I was not that religious or spiritual back then, I didn't know that it was God embracing me. It was so beautiful.

Three years later my husband saw a program on TV and they were talking about the very same thing. We both realized there was a name attached to my experience (OBE) and that others experienced this wonderful phenomena also.

LINDA MARIE

Joining My Husband in Spirit

I had a wonderfully sweet experience that was not a dream, which I would like to share.

One night while meditating, I happened to find myself suddenly sitting at my sewing machine in the basement where I use it. I heard someone coming down the stairs and wondered who it was. As I turned around to look, I heard my deceased husband say, "Yeah it's me!" I was so surprised to see him, and as I looked at him, he disappeared for just a second and then I could see him plainly again.

He was carrying something in his hands and set it down on the floor. He next walked over and hugged and kissed me and was gone again! If you are wondering what the gift was that he brought me, it was a beautiful handmade vanity bench that he had made for me in Heaven. I know this because he told me on an earlier occasion that he liked to "make things" since he passed over. I was experiencing an out of body experience (OBE) when this happened.

ELAINE STEGALL

The White Room

I was a foot reflexologist and an energy healer at a woman's medical center when I had a wonderful OBE. One day I was at work and was nearing the completion of a Reflexology session for a client of mine. My client was a sweet woman, who had been taking care of her physically and mentally challenged daughter. The woman was exhausted from the strain of it all. I felt, in addition to the Reflexology session, that she could also use some of the Holy Spirit's healing energy going into her body. While keeping my hands on her feet, as she lay in a reclining green chair in my office, I started to pray silently for her. I asked the Holy Spirit to please send in His healing energy to this woman. And I felt God answering, "Yes," as my hands began to heat up and pulsate with the Holy Spirit's healing energy coursing through my hands and going into my client, who was now peacefully sleeping.

While my eyes were closed and I was concentrating on this healing, I suddenly found myself in a room that was filled with vivid white Light. The white Light was perfectly and evenly distributed throughout the entire room—no shadows or variations in intensity or shadings of the Light. This white Light was like nothing I had ever seen before. It didn't resemble sunlight, nor artificial light either.

I found myself floating high above in this "special room of Light," and as I glanced downward, I noticed the room was empty except for two people and a reclining green chair. The two people below me were my client and myself! I saw my physical body holding the feet of my client, who was still sleeping in the reclining green chair. My client and I both appeared small, as if I were watching this scene from a distance high above—which I was.

While continuing to watch my client and myself below me, I was slowly and peacefully floating above and around the room in a circular motion, as if I were riding on an invisible carousel going around in slow motion. I was not frightened, but intrigued. I knew instinctively that something very, very special was happening to me and that Holy Spirit had arranged for this awesome experience.

Eventually, I opened my eyes and found I was now back in my physical body, still holding this woman's feet. The whole experience was surreal, yet extremely peaceful. I knew I had just had my first out of body experience (OBE). I felt this is what it must be like to be in our spiritual bodies, without being weighed down by our physical ones. It was a wonderful feeling and I feel so very blessed to have experienced this. Thank You, God, for giving me a little glimpse into what awaits us in the heavens with You.

CHRISTINE DUMINIAK

Flying with the Clouds

I was recovering from pneumonia and was still pretty fatigued. While recuperating, I was doing some work on my computer and trying to download music from the Internet. As I waited for the music to download, I decided to take a nap.

I am not sure if I was just falling asleep or getting ready to wake up, but I must have been in a twilight sleep. I remember feeling a pulling sensation, and felt my spirit come apart from my physical body. In my mind, I realized that I was separate from my body. At first, I slowly started to float upwards towards the ceiling and then through the roof of the house.

Once outside, my body kept floating upwards faster and faster. I remember seeing the trees as I passed them. The next thing I knew, I was as high as the clouds in the sky. I was taking in the beauty of the sunshine mixing in with the clouds. Never once was I afraid or fearful. I had the most peaceful feeling.

While I was high in the sky, I kept telling myself to really look around at everything that I was seeing and to make a mental note, so that I would never forget what this experience felt like. A part of me also wondered if I would meet up with my fiancé who had just crossed over the previous year; unfortunately, that didn't happen. I remember that I had several thoughts, one being I wondered if this is what "death" felt like. Secondly, I remember feeling so much peace; I didn't want to return to my physical body.

I can't tell you how long this experience lasted, but I can say that I had a great amount of peace when I woke up. This experience has eased my fear of what I may experience when I die. I hope it helps others not to be afraid to "die" either.

LAURA

* * *

AFTER-DEATH COMMUNICATIONS

* * *

CHAPTER 22

Phones, Texts, Caller IDs & Answering Machines

Some of our loved ones seem to like to keep in touch the good old-fashioned way! Can you hear me now?

Whaddup?

My son Braden Talbott Lindholdt died on March 11, 2001, in a kayaking accident, the details of which are still unclear. He was with his best friend Jim, both twenty years old, and their bodies were never found. Of course this was, and most likely will be, the greatest devastation ever to hit either of our families.

I was in so much grief initially that many of my prayers for Braden were, "Please bring him back."

After a couple of months, however, I was able to pray about more logical issues related to Braden; one of which was for him to send me a sign, any sign, many signs, to let me know he was fine and happy. As a result, God has more than answered my prayers. One of the best ways in which he has contacted me has been through our digital answering machine.

Normally, after a message is left on our answering machine, the date and time is announced automatically at the very end of the caller's message. However, when Braden leaves his messages, his messages come AFTER the date and time announcement is made. An area where the messages are not designed to record. It is a small static-filled area right before the machine cuts out.

I got his first message in August. He simply said, "Whaddup?" just like he always did when greeting me. I listened to it a few times, and even though it sounded exactly like Braden, I couldn't bring myself to believe it. I thought I was going bonkers, and deleted it. I got the second message a few weeks later. He said, "Ehhhhhh!" a hilarious sound he used to make in mock embarrassment. It was almost as if he was telling me he realized I had erased him! Even though this was so indicative of his personality and was his unique way of expressing himself, I still deleted it as well, thinking I had gone "clear around the bend." But the thought of him trying to send me these messages wouldn't leave my mind.

A couple of weeks later, he left what I think was his third message. This one was a clear question: "Mom?" as if he were again saying that it was really him and asking if I heard him. Well, that one I saved, along with the next one that came on October 25, 2001.

I got home and there was Braden on the machine again. He was a rap artist, so he rapped, "You aren't home. Hey, Mom, I have to say that I don't know why!" It's so clearly his voice that even his skeptic friends and relatives have had to concede that it really was him.

A few weeks later, Jim's mom, Mary Jo, came over, (As I mentioned, Jim was lost in the kayaking accident also.) After she listened to the messages from Braden, she prayed right then and there to God to have Jim learn how to leave one too. Not more than thirty minutes after Mary Jo's prayer, the phone rang. I told Mary Jo I wasn't going to answer it, as we were busy chatting. And guess what? This time it was her son Jim who left a message on the answering machine. He said, "I'll come again." We believe this was in direct response to Mary Jo's prayer thirty minutes earlier.

We thank God for these messages from our boys. The comfort that these signs have given us have helped to ease our grief and remind us they are very much alive and well.

VICKI TALBOTT AND MARY JO

The Fight and the Phone Call

Even though Andre and I were divorced, we were still close friends when he passed over. Around the first anniversary of his death, our daughter Hannah was having major behavioral problems in school and at home. In the past, she had thrown some huge temper tantrums!

One day after school, she came home in a particularly bad mood. There was no dealing with her. She was crying and saying all kinds of things that were unreal. I kept sending her to her room, as it was the only way to deal with her when she was like this, but she kept coming back downstairs hurling accusations and untruths at me. After doing this for about thirty minutes, I had lost patience and was feeling angry with her. My baby twins were now crying and the whole house was in an uproar. I felt so helpless at that point. I just wanted her to stop this upsetting behavior.

I also got angry at Andre for not being here when I needed him, and I said out loud to Andre, "If you are really here and you really want to help, please intervene and help me. I don't want to feel this way, and Hannah obviously can't stop herself at this point." Afterwards, I sat down on the couch and started to cry out of pure frustration.

Then the phone suddenly rang. I thought, "Oh great, it's my mom calling to invite Hannah over and I'm gonna have to say, no, and most likely another temper tantrum will follow." By the time I got to the phone it had already rung three times. Our phone has a caller ID on the handset. I looked at the caller ID, and there wasn't a number or name listed. I thought that was weird because something always shows up.

As I finished that thought, *our* phone number came up on the caller ID! I got the chills, picked up the receiver and said, "Hello?" I heard the strangest static I've ever heard. There was no answer to my hello. I looked at the caller ID again, and sure enough our own phone number was actually showing. But how could that be?

I asked "Hello?" again, but still no answer, just strange sounding static. I hung up the phone and sat down on the couch dumbfounded. Then it hit me! I had asked Andre to help and he did! I sat there with my mouth hanging open. Hannah came down the stairs and asked, "What's wrong, Mommy?" I said, "Honey, you won't believe this." I told her what had just happened and we hugged over the incredible phone call incident. Consequently, the whole tantrum came to a halt. I thanked God, and I was in a happy stupor for the rest of the evening.

As background, when Hannah was little, Andre used to make the phone ring in our house so she could have fun answering it. So on this particular hectic night, Andre once again somehow made our phone ring in the midst of all the chaos.

Since Andre's passing, this was the one and only time this has ever happened to us. I told my husband the whole story when he came home later. He came to the same conclusion that I did—it was Andre. I had asked for his help and he had given it to me.

I went to bed that night and prayed and thanked God for Andre's intervention and thanked God for not giving up on me. This incident opened me up to many more wonderful awakenings that were to follow. I have never looked at the world the same way again.

AMY DEMOSS

The Hole-In-One Text Message

The day after Christmas in 1997, it was an abnormally warm winter day here in Pennsylvania. So my husband and I took advantage of it by going golfing at Neshaminy Vally Golf Course.

Amazingly during our golf outing, I had one of those very rare hole-in-ones! I had never had one before and my husband and I couldn't believe our eyes as the ball hit the green, rolled along and then disappeared into the cup after only one shot. We were high-fiving and celebrating!

Back in 1997, I was golfing mostly with a group of women once a week. Because our kids were younger, and my husband was still working, it was hard for us to go golfing together. So it was so thrilling to be able to have my husband share and witness this exciting event with me. We were both ecstatic! We marveled that it should happen on one of those few times we were out actually golfing together. What are the odds?

In 1997, I was not aware of ADCs, So I didn't realize that this hole-in-one was a gift from my husband's parents who had both passed over some years earlier. However, since 1998 I have become spiritually aware, and I have had many ADCs that I now recognize to be from my mother and father-in-law.

Fast forward to 2014. Something inexplicable happened again at that same golf course, Neshaminy Valley! My husband and I were both golfing together when my mind suddenly turned to that marvelous day back in 1997 when I had that hole-in-one. I smiled thinking about my in-laws' part in it. When my husband and I were finished golfing, I looked at my cell phone to see if I had any messages. My phone showed that I had a text message from my husband at 3:30 p.m., while we were out together golfing! Even though there was no actual message typed in, the phone showed that it was his cell phone number and his name that had sent me a blank text message.

So I asked him if he had sent me a text at 3:30 p.m.? He said, "No! I was with you. Why would I send you a text message?"

I laughed and said, "It was from your parents! I had been thinking about them today and the hole-in-one that I now realize that they had arranged for me the day after Christmas 17 years ago!"

This text was not accidently sent from my husband's phone either, as six different buttons would have had to have been pressed in order to send me that blank text message. LOL! Even my husband was amazed! What a great validation of my in-laws' participation in my hole-in-one!

CHRISTINE DUMINIAK

Happy Easter From Our Children

I have prayed and have received many after-death communications from my young son Nicola since he passed over at the age of six years and two months. There is one in particular I would like to share here.

One Easter night a friend of mine, who also lost his child, phoned me at home. We chatted for a while, both from our home telephones–not cell phones. After we hung up, a few minutes later my home phone rang again; it was once again my friend, asking me why I had recalled him now on his cell phone?

I was very puzzled. Not only because I had *not* called him back, but also I did not even have or know his cell phone number! He was shocked because he said his cellular phone rang, but no one was on the line, and it had my home phone number listed on it as the incoming call!

I went upstairs to check another telephone in my house. This telephone has a flash memory that works without batteries, but it will not record a number dialed, unless you actually lift the receiver and make a call. And to my astonishment, there was my friend's cell phone number recorded on that telephone, showing that a call was made to his cell phone from a telephone in my house, but no one had dialed that number from our house! I know no one could have intercepted my telephone lines from outside of my home because, if this had been the case, his cell phone number would not have been recorded on my phone in my house, the way it was.

Just to double check, later on I called our phone company in my hometown in Italy, and they told me that no charges are on my bill from a phone call on Easter night that were made to my friend's cell phone! And my friend also found out that there were no charges found on his cell phone bill coming from my home phone number either! And since a technician confirmed that it is impossible to make a call from a home phone to a cell phone, without it showing up in their computer system (which it did not), the only explanation is that a spirit (not a human) phoned both of us that night. Surely this unexplained phone call was a Happy Easter from both of our children who are Home with God.

Don't worry about not receiving ADCs from your deceased loved ones. They can communicate with us in some of the most remarkable ways if we are open to the spirit world.

CLAUDIO PISANI, M.D.

You Called Me! No, You Called Me!

My baby brother Ashley went Home to God at the age of twenty-three, on January 17, 2002. I missed him so very much. He used to call me a zillion times a day and I missed that contact with him.

One night about 2:45 in the morning, I was going crazy. I could not sleep. I was crying and thinking about my brother Ashley. I started to pray, "Lord, help me. Please let me know if my brother Ashley is okay. Also, Lord, please watch over my mother. I am worried about her. Please, Lord, send me a sign. If Ashley can come down, let him, my precious Lord, in Jesus' name."

After my prayer, the phone rang. I picked it up, but there was no one on the other end. I looked at the caller ID, and my mother's number was listed. I thought perhaps she was having a bad night, too, so I called her right back. The phone rang twice. The thought went through my mind that, since mom just called me, she should have answered by now. So I hung up the phone not wanting to disturb her.

A second later she called me back. She said, "Did you just call me?" I replied, "No, Mother, you just called me first, and I was just calling you back." My mother said she had not dialed my number at all! Then I felt my brother's presence. It was like he was standing right in front of me saying, "OK, you two will be all right for the night now."

You see, my mother and I were both having a bad night missing Ashley, and neither of us wanted to call each other for solace because it was so late. But Ashley took care of that matter for us. We knew that Ashley was watching over us. Coincidentally, 2:45 a.m. was the estimated time of Ashley's death. I had prayed in Jesus' name and He answered my prayers. Amen.

Not too long after this mysterious phone call incident, I had another similar one. My phone rang, and when I answered the phone the woman said, "Bonos. May I help you?" I asked, "Why did you call me?" She replied, "I did not call you, you called me!"

When I informed her that I did not call her, that she called me, I think she thought I was a bit crazy. But the really interesting thing is this—Bonos is the store where by brother Ashley worked for about six years! I believe my brother Ashley had rung my phone and Bonos' phone at the same time and connected us to each other in order to get my attention and to say, "Hello, Sis."

TERI LYNN POWELL

The ADC I Requested

My mom Carmen Martinez passed on April 8, 2003, which was also my son's third birthday. My ADC was about a week after my mother's death, and it was late in the evening. I was doing my usual cleaning up after dinner and putting my two small children to bed.

After this, I sat down and began to recite the rosary. When I finished the rosary I asked for a sign to let me know that my mom was okay. I said, "Let the phone ring so I know you're okay."

The time I went to bed was about 12:30 a.m. The phone rang at 1 a.m. I answered the phone and there was just silence. Even though there was no one there, the "phone rang" just as I had requested of my mom.

I believe in my heart that my mom was answering my request for a sign, to ease my mind, by letting me know she was, indeed, fine being back Home with the Lord.

PATTIE ALCUS

* * *

CHAPTER 23

Scents

There is a uniqueness about scents that can bring back memories of a loved one. When they visit us using this particular style, they must be standing beside us smiling with us, as we recognize their presence.

The Scent of My Grandmother

We called our grandmother, Welita, which is short for grandmother in Spanish. Welita was one of the sweetest grandmothers in the world. Don't we love them so? She loved all of her grandchildren, and each one of us thought we were her favorite. When she passed, I packed her belongings, and her little treasure was a plastic bag filled with pictures of each one of her grandchildren.

One of my greatest regrets is the day she called and asked me to bring my baby over to visit her, as she was feeling lonely. But I did not go. Instead I showed up a week later to find her asleep forever. I was with my baby daughter and my screams reached up to the heavens. If you have the chance to show someone you love them today—do it.

The day of Welita's funeral on a Saturday afternoon at 1 p.m., the doorbell rang. I was on my way up the stairs, but stopped and waited to see who was there, as my husband opened the door. But no one was there. We looked at each other thinking that was odd. Suddenly the house filled up with the heaviest scent of flowers. The scent traveled. My husband seemed in shock because the scent became heavier and heavier. Then the scent turned into the smell of the clothes that I had packed from Welita's apartment a few days earlier. It was very definitely her scent.

Thicker and thicker the scent became as it passed right by me, traveling up the stairs. I called to my husband, "It's Welita!" I followed the scent. The scent stopped at my baby daughter's bedroom and totally disappeared. Welita knew I'd recognize her scent and her visit to see my baby. She knew that I had deeply regretted not coming by to see her earlier when she requested before she passed. I believe she wanted to take that guilt from me.

Eleven years had gone by since her passing and her afterlife visit. It was now October of 1997. My cousin Angie had been sick with cancer. Because we lived on opposite coasts and did not often keep in touch, I had no idea she was in her last days. As I was sleeping on this October morning, when I heard three loud knocks on my door. I jumped up out of my sleep and looked at the clock It was 7:30 a.m. No one was at the door, and I wondered if this was a spirit communication.

During that same month of October, I was typing at my computer when, suddenly, a familiar scent surrounded me. I thought I recognized it to be my grandmother's, but wasn't sure so I kept typing away. When the scent grew thicker, I opened the windows to see if the scent was coming from the outside, but it wasn't. As the scent continued to grow heavier, I positively recognized it to be my grandmother's scent. Welita had arrived. But why eleven years later?

A few days later I found out why. I received the news that my cousin Angie had passed. I realized that my grandmother had visited me to tell me that my "partner-in-crime," my childhood friend, who was also my best friend, and whom I adored, was with my grandmother and now okay, as are all of my family who have gone before me. Welita taught me that our loved ones will communicate with us in a manner that they know we will recognize is from them.

JENNY FLORES

Lots and Lots of Flowers

When our dad passed over in 2000, people asked us if we would prefer flowers or a donation to a charitable cause for his funeral. My mother choose to forgo the flowers in lieu of a donation. However, after the funeral was over, my mother lamented her decision a bit because she felt there were not enough flowers at the service to honor our dad. Mom talked about this for months. It really bothered her a lot.

When our mother passed four years later, people asked me, "Flowers or a donation?" Remembering how my mother felt about the lack of flowers at our dad's funeral, and knowing she would be attending her own funeral in spirit, I said, "Flowers!" I had visions of my mother *haunting* me if there were not enough flowers at her funeral too!

The funeral was very emotional for me, as I wrote and gave the Eulogy for our mom. I wasn't sure how I was going to get through it, but with God's help and with both of my parents' spiritual help, I did.

When I returned home from that exhausting day, I immediately took a nap in my bedroom. I was so wiped out physically and emotionally. As I started to awaken from my nap, I noticed a very, very strong floral scent all around me. Yet there were no flowers in the room or anywhere close by. I was elated. I knew I was receiving an acknowledgement and a thank you from my dear mother for all the lovely flowers at her beautiful funeral. I will never forget how gratifying and joyful this floral ADC scent from my mother felt. It brought a smile to my grieving heart.

CHRISTINE DUMINIAK

Mom's Yellow Tank Top

My mother passed away November of 1981, almost nineteen years before this ADC happened. About a month after she died, I was going through her dresser and I pulled out her favorite bright yellow tank top. I put it to my face and could smell her so strongly; it was like she was standing before me. I never wanted to wash that shirt because it was so filled with the smell of Mom—her cologne, her hair, her skin, and her life. Over the past nineteen years, I recall standing in her room in my parents' house and holding that tank top only a few times, maybe three or four total, and I have never been revisited by that fragrance after the first time I smelled it a month after her passing. This is significant to illustrate that the memory was not recalled frequently.

On September 21, 2000, I walked out of my office building at 2 p.m. I was on my way to pick up my father to take him to the doctor. He had not been feeling well and had been depressed lately. As I stepped out of the office door and into the sunlight, I got this overwhelming scent and I recognized it immediately. As I walked toward my car I was inhaling as deeply as I could because I wanted to be sure of it. Immediately, I was mentally taken back to the bedroom, the dresser drawer, and the yellow tank top. It was the exact smell of nineteen years earlier. It was quintessential Mom, her substance, her spirit, her entity. She was there with me and I was not alarmed. I smiled thinking it was dandy she was going with us to the doctor.

I had no idea of the real significance of her presence. I was about to learn that at 1:55 p.m. my father had shot and killed himself.

When I pulled up in front of Dad's house and saw the squad cars and emergency services, immediately I thought of the fragrance from the parking lot just minutes earlier. I knew why she had come, and because of that, I had it in me to remain calm. I had been given warning. She had told me in her own way. Because of this, I had to know that Dad was all right, no matter what was going on inside that house, no matter what the outside conditions might otherwise reveal. "There is no power in conditions," that was Mom's message to me that afternoon.

ELAINE

Merry Christmas

My father Stanley passed on November 17, 1994. As you can imagine the holidays following dad's November passing were so very difficult without his dynamic and loving presence.

It was our first Christmas without him and my mother and I were in my house waiting for other family members to arrive. In my holiday-decorated dining room, I noticed suddenly there was a very strong, lovely floral scent filling the air, yet, there was nothing alive or scented in the decorations that could account for this extremely strong fragrance.

I called my mother into the room and asked her if she had placed something scented into the centerpiece. She had not!

Nothing in the house could have accounted for this beautiful, sweet-smelling floral bouquet scent we smelled! Nothing but dad. He was there showing us he was with us!

CAROL

Clove Cigarettes

My son Ashley died on January 17, 2002; he was twenty-three years old and my baby. I found him in his bed and I was devastated. My life totally changed from that moment on. I did not think I could bear the pain, but God's grace seemed to hold me during those days when I needed it the most. Ashley's death was so unexpected that each night I prayed, "God, let me know he is okay."

Well, Ashley had been gone about a month and I could not sleep, which was normal for me since he died. My husband was snoring beside me and it was 2:30 in the morning. I closed my eyes and tried to will myself to relax. All of a sudden there was this overwhelming smell of "clove" cigarettes. Now Ashley smoked these things, and I hated the way they smelled because they were so strong. I sat up in bed and the "scent" was all around me. It stayed for about a minute. It was peaceful and comforting. I knew then that God had answered a mother's prayer. Ashley was A-OK. He still had that sense of humor. He knew that was a scent that no one else would be associated with. This time though, it was a blessing.

Since Ashley's passing we have cleaned Ashley's room several times with Pine-Sol. We have lit candles in there, yet Ashley's scent is still there. We are not trying to get rid of it, but just regular cleaning as most people do. Nothing eliminates it. So I just leave it alone now and dust. When you walk in, you can smell his soul scent as I call it. We all have one. There are neither clothes in there nor anything else that is personal, so the scent does not come from anything in the room, other than Ashley. I thank God for this comfort. I would go in there most days and just "smell" him. God is good! I will see my son again one day, and I know I will hold him again and see that wonderful smile.

DONNA BOWMAN

* * *

* * *

CHAPTER 24

Suicides & Afterlife Visits

> Suicide often leaves the ones left behind feeling horribly guilty and reeling over a loved one's drastic actions. If you desire to help someone you found out left by their own hand, please pray for them. Our prayers for them will help them tremendously to forgive themselves before God. When you receive a comforting afterlife sign from someone who has taken their own life, you can be at peace knowing they are at peace.

Why? Why? Why?

After the suicide of Tina Maria, my daughter Nately's friend, she prayed for a sign that Tina Maria would not be punished for taking her own life. Tina Maria had suffered ongoing abuse in her family, which she had never shared with her mother. The sign my daughter received, in answer to her prayers, was a dream visit.

It was Easter Sunday morning. The day we celebrate eternal life because Jesus Christ rose from the dead. Early in the morning I ran to my fifteen-year-old daughter's bedroom because I heard her crying. She sobbed hysterically as I entered her room, "Mommy, Mommy, why did Tina Maria have to do this? Why did she kill herself?" "Tina Maria! Why did you do this?" She sobbed uncontrollably. I felt so sorry for my daughter as I searched for the right words to comfort her. And then she began to tell me about her dream.

She explained that Tina Maria and she were together in their high school hallway. Nately spoke to her and asked her, "Why did you do this, Tina Maria? This was so selfish of you." Tina Maria hung her head low and nodded. She wasn't proud of what she had done.

Nately continued on with the dream. She asked her, "Why did you do this, Tina Maria? We were going to play." (They had made plans to go to the mall.) Tina Maria said, "Don't worry. We'll get to play again." Tina Maria hugged and kissed Nately and said, "I love you." And then she left. In the dream Nately began to cry hysterically and she threw herself into the arms of another kid next to her as she collapsed onto the floor.

Then Tina Maria returned in the dream. She had different clothes on this time. She was wearing a red and white sweat suit with a beautiful design that Nately had never seen before. Nately exclaimed, "Tina Maria! You're back! You changed your clothes!" Nately got up off the floor and Tina Maria hugged her tightly again.

Tina Maria said, "I love you. I have to go now." Nately begged her, "Let me walk you out, Tina Maria." But Tina Maria pointed to the direction she was going and said, "That's okay. I know my way now." And she disappeared. And the dream ended there.

I wanted to comfort my daughter, to assure her that although Tina Maria at fifteen years old had taken her life, she was surely alive as this was the PROMISE OF GOD. He gave His only Son, so that death would be defeated and there would be eternal life. As I sat on my daughter's bed consoling her I said, "Nately, she just told you goodbye, and what is today? It's Easter Sunday. This is the day that Jesus Christ rose from the dead. As Christ has risen, so shall we. Remember that. She's alive. She was here to let you know she is alive."

After Tina Maria had taken her life, her friends had many after-death contacts from her. There were telephone calls, pager codes inputted with 1-4-3 that meant in their teen language "I love you." There were also frequent dreams to her friends with little messages. In one dream she asked a favor of one of her best friends. She said, "Go visit my mother."

Years have passed and from time to time I ask my daughter, "Do you dream of Tina Maria anymore?" She answers, "No." And I reminded her, "That's because she came that Easter Sunday to let you know that she was fine, and she too has risen."

God bless you, Tina Maria. We know you can hear us.

JENNY FLORES & NATELY

Come For A Walk With Me

My fiancé Andrew suffered from bipolar disorder and had taken his own life suddenly and unexpectedly.

I wanted to see my fiancé Andrew one last time before his cremation. I felt strongly he was waiting for me. It had been nearly three days since his passing and his neighbor wished to take me to Andrew's viewing, as none of the family wanted to see him. I just had to say goodbye and also to see that it was real. It was so hard to believe.

On the way to the chapel, it was as if someone was tapping a Morse code signal on my hand. It was quite strong, between my thumb and my first finger. It stopped while I was viewing Andrew and started up again as soon as we left. The tapping stopped when we got back to Andrew's place and then started up again in the afternoon on the way to the cremation. It then stopped altogether and it has not happened again since.

A few days later, I was supposed to take the wreath that was on the coffin. Inadvertently it got locked in the garage and I needed to go to the neighbor's for the key. On the way over there, I passed by the tree where Andrew had ended his life and I whispered, "Come for a walk with me." I had to cross a cultivated paddock and took off my shoes, as we always used to do, so our feet could feel the earth.

I was close to reaching the other side of the paddock when I heard footsteps behind me. I turned around to look, but no one was there. Very distinctly I heard Andrew say, "I will always be one step behind you."

As I was returning, Andrew's sister was coming to meet me and she said she saw this incredible glow near me. Then, as she hugged me, she said she felt an indescribable feeling of love that she felt was Andrew coming through her to cuddle me.

Love and light.

KATH MCLACHLAN

Healing From Suicide

My dear friend Bryan committed suicide twenty-five years ago. He was suffering from post-traumatic stress syndrome after serving in the Vietnam War.

After a seventeen-year absence of communication, I received an after-death communication from Bryan. It was a very loud and clear auditory voice mentioning John. When I heard the voice, I knew immediately that this was my friend and my love Bryan, whose death by suicide had shattered my soul twenty-five years previously, and that the John he referred to was a young man in my life for only a few months. John and I had an instant rapport and I already loved him like a brother.

Soon after Bryan's audio message to me, John came to me extremely upset that his ex-boyfriend was threatening suicide. I knew I was not only being given the opportunity to help John with what I had learned about dealing with suicide, but also an opportunity to heal myself. You see, I was stuck in repressed and unfinished grief and needed to move forward.

I took the hint and attended a suicide survivor's support group. I heard myself offering these words, "It's not your fault!" to a family suffering a recent loss of a family member to suicide. The message I delivered to them, also came through loud and clear to me as well, that I was not to blame myself either. After this revelation, I was able to finally complete my healing process.

This after-death communication also led to my taking the necessary steps to have Bryan honored in a ceremony in Washington, DC for Vietnam Veterans, whose deaths were a result of their service in the Vietnam arena, even though they were not killed in an actual battle. I know Bryan led me to get this done because, when I was trying to make a decision about whether or not to follow through on the ceremony idea by calling his sister about it, I felt Bryan's presence with me with a love that filled my being. I knew he was giving me the go-ahead to call his sister to start the process. This Vietnam veterans' ceremony was very healing not only for me but I believe for Bryan's family as well.

ROBIN

The First Father's Day

It was the first Father's Day since Daddy took his life in September of 2000. Almost nine months had gone by. I was driving and thinking about the fact that it was the first Father's Day. I really wanted to think about Daddy, to remember him, and to give him some sort of mental tribute today. I felt sorry that I didn't think I could. There is only one "first" Father's Day, after your father passes over. Yet I didn't think I could dwell on this particular Father's Day because of my mother-in-law PJ's cancer, as well as my husband's understandable moodiness, and other worldly circumstances deserving and requiring attention. We say that "there are no big deals," yet my life seems to have been defined from one big deal to the next.

While driving I remembered that I was angry with Dad for not letting me help him more when he had breathing problems. I didn't think he tried hard enough to find out what was wrong with him. After all, he wouldn't even go to the doctor to get a diagnosis about his breathing problem, or his extreme anxiety about what it could be. "We'll get a diagnosis, then a treatment plan." I would tell him. Shortly before he killed himself he teased me saying, "First a diagnosis, then a treatment plan! When I die that's what you're gonna put on my tombstone, Here lies Jim. Wouldn't get a diagnosis, wouldn't get a treatment plan." We laughed but I told him, "Don't you think I won't!"

And so, when Dad took his life, I felt cheated. It is true that God must enjoy a sense of humor and undoubtedly Dad is howling madly at the current set of circumstances. My mother- in-law is newly diagnosed with lung cancer and tomorrow begins the merry-go-round of radiation and chemotherapy for seven and a half weeks. After that who can say what comes next? First the diagnosis, then the treatment plan. Yes indeed I can hear Dad now, "OK, Sister, here you go! Have at it!"

So on Father's Day, while driving in my car, I was feeling sorry for myself and pondering the irony of this, I would be able to help my mother-in-law, but not my own dad. Again, I made the commitment to double my efforts on her behalf. I would do my best for her anyway because I love her, but I will double my efforts because I will remember Daddy and how angry I was that I could not do for him. I will double my efforts on her behalf in his memory and this should benefit all of us. It will allow me to service out the anger towards my dad, and it will assist PJ in her dailies. Boom-boom. Everybody wins and my dad Jim gets a big laugh. I also vowed to choose to be kind rather than right. I also vowed to keep my mouth closed when I am tempted to give unsolicited advice.

While driving around on Father's Day, I leaned over to change the radio station. I suddenly heard the sweet little song played at Dad's memorial, "Love Without End, Amen" by George Strait. The same song my dad and I had found a few days before he took his life that (I think) gave him permission to do the deed. Or, at the very least, those lyrics may have lessened his fear of going to Hell to the extent he could actually pull the trigger.

When he read the lyrics, we cried together, and he told me his greatest fear in life was going to Hell, without giving me a hint that he was thinking about taking his own life. As I think back, I feel like he had been contemplating this action for several days, but at the time I had no idea. What else in his life would have made him a candidate for this feared damnation of Hell? Nothing, but still, he was afraid.

The lyrics to "Love Without End, Amen" are about a man who dreamt he'd died last night and found himself standing outside the gates of Heaven. Suddenly he was struck with terror and bewilderment, as he realized there must be some mistake, because if God knew half the things he'd done, he'd never be allowed admittance. Immediately following these thoughts, the man in the dream heard a booming voice from the other side of the gates. The voice repeated what his own father had told him many times as a boy, when he had gotten into trouble. It's a truth his father said was kept between them. It's that daddies don't just love their children only when they're good—it is unceasing and everlasting with no beginning and no end. It simply is.

In the preceding nine months, I had only heard that song on the radio once. It was the six-month anniversary of his death, and now I heard it again on this Father's Day, the first Father's Day, June 17, 2001. This was not a coincidence. It was Daddy telling me I am on the right track, that he is not disappointed in me, that he is still around, and that he loves me. He was acknowledging this first Father's Day because he knew I selfishly wanted someone to recognize my loss and fearing the day would pass and no one would do that for me. On that first Father's Day, there is nothing else that would have been more convincing to me that my dad was with me, other than that song. Had he appeared in front of my eyes, I might have mistrusted it as a hallucination. He knew that and chose the ADC that would speak to me unquestionably.

ELAINE

He Still Loves Music

I pray regularly for my dear nephew and thank God when I get an ADC. Here is my story: My dear nephew Rudy committed suicide. He was like a son to me. He used to run away from home and hide when he could no longer take the emotional abuse he was getting from his dad. Sometimes he would go to his friends' houses and sometimes to my home to hide. I tried being a haven for Rudy a number of times by hiding him in my back bedroom. Eventually, my roommate brought up the fact that we could get in trouble for harboring a minor, if Rudy's parents found out and reported us to the police. I did not want to go against my roommate, even though my heart desperately wanted to hide my nephew when the going got rough. So out of respect for my roommate's wishes, I no longer was a place of refuge for Rudy. When Rudy had nowhere else to run to, he would spend the night in a building that he knew would be empty at night time.

A few weeks after Rudy's suicide, I started having these awful guilt feelings. I felt that I wasn't there enough for my nephew when he was having hard times. I felt I should have gone against my roommate's wishes, and that I should have continued to take Rudy into my home. The guilt feelings had risen to the point where I could hardly function anymore, and it was getting too hard to make it through the day. I would pray to God asking Him to please help me make it through each day!

One day I called one of Rudy's best friends and talked to her about how badly I was feeling. She made me feel better and a lot more at ease. That day after work, I was driving to pick up my son, and all of a sudden, I smelled the scent of the same candle that I burn in my bedroom. The scent was soooo strong. It was as if I were burning that candle in my truck at that very instant. I cried because I knew it was Rudy and I knew that he knew about how badly I was feeling. I knew he was telling me, "Please don't have any guilt feelings, I love you." I cried in the truck and held my hand to my chest and said, "Thank you, Rudy, for coming to me and totally easing my mind," and I said, "Thank you, God, for letting him come to me!"

Another ADC I received from Rudy had to do with music on two different occasions. These music ADCs happened a week apart. I woke up early one morning and I heard a song playing so strongly in my head that it sounded like there was a stereo inside it. I could hear the instrumental and the voice, as if I had headphones on. I heard the song by U2 "Peace on Earth" and it lasted for about thirty seconds to a minute.

A week before the same thing happened, where I could hear the song playing loudly inside of my head. The song that Rudy played for me then was by REM, called "Everybody Hurts." Rudy and I liked the same kind of music and still do!

CINDY B.

* * *

CHAPTER 25

Visions of Adults

Spirits can show themselves inside of our mind's eye or outside of ourselves. What a thrill it is to get to see them again this way! God is good!

I Can't Believe I Just Did That!

My brother Brian was just a young man when he very suddenly got called back Home to God. He was my baby brother, adorable, and I just loved him so. He was a constant presence in my life and around my family. I pray for him often and I pray to get after-death communications from him too.

One night I had gotten out of bed to get a glass of milk for my little boy Matt. I was walking back from the kitchen, with the glass of milk in my hand, in a somewhat sleepy state. As I started walking towards the hallway from the kitchen to the bedroom, I noticed my brother Brian leaning up against the wall. His arms were folded over, and a cute half-smile, half-grin covered his face. I looked at him and put my hand up to wave and I said, "Hey, Bri!" as I walked right by him, just as if he were still here physically! It wasn't until a few minutes later that I realized that he had passed over a number of months ago, and I was talking to his spirit! I said to myself, I can't believe I just did that! I can't believe I walked right by the spirit of my brother, as if his visit were an everyday occurrence!

Brian's unexpected visit and my nonchalant response still make me laugh out loud every time I think of it. It warms my very heart and soul. We are still very much brother and sister and he can still make me laugh. I just love that brother of mine!

LAURI

Her Face in the Clouds

Jackie was more like a sister to me than a sister-in-law. When she passed over from cancer recently, I missed her more than I could begin to say. She is constantly on my mind and in my prayers, and I have prayed to have contact from her. My prayers have been answered because she has sent many ADCs my way to let me know she is thinking about me too.

There was a special sign that I received from Jackie that I would like to share with you. I had stepped out my back door to let my dog in. As I looked out, I noticed that the sky was a strange color—well, strange for our area of the world in the Midwest. It was a reddish-blue color. Instead of going back into the house, I decided to go out and give the heavens above more than a passing glance.

As I was peering up at the sky, my eye caught this one particular cloud. It looked pretty normal, but then all of sudden I could see it changing. As I watched the cloud change shape, I saw the outline of Jackie's face start to form. It reminded me of that gadget you see in the store that, when you press your face or hand against it, it leaves an impression from the warmth of it. The cloud formation kept getting clearer and sharper. I started to get tunnel vision. I couldn't sense anything else around me or hear anything.

I asked Jackie if it was really her in that cloud, and I heard her say, "Yes." She told me that she is happy and to please stop worrying about her. Then the cloud started to dissolve. It wasn't floating away like you normally see with clouds, instead it just started to dissolve. I said, "Please don't go." and just that quickly it started to come back. The outline of her face reappeared.

I tried closing my eyes to say a quick prayer, but I kept seeing these flashes of light. This phenomenon could have been just from staring at the sky too long. Anyway, I said, "OK, I will just watch." As Jackie's cloud disappeared, a series of clouds appeared. It was just a long set of clouds. It reminded me of a Morse code line (dot dot dot dash) or just (dot dot dash). I don't know Morse code, but I do know that some people from the Prayer Wave For After-Death Communication Message Board, where I post, have this connection with hearing Morse code in their ears from their loved ones. I asked Jackie if this Morse code type of cloud formation was for someone else and she said, "Yes."

I can't tell you the feeling that came over me. When you receive these ADCs it is awesome. Time stood still for me for several minutes.

Thanks Jac, you are simply the best!

SUE

He Kissed Me Again

Since my dear fiancé Mark crossed over very unexpectedly, I have been blessed to receive many different types of ADCs. These have been in the form of dreams, visions in my mind's eye, spiritual appearances outside of my mind, sensing a presence, feeling touches, many music ADCs, cloud images, and dragonfly and butterfly ADCs too. I would like to share with you a few that I received in just one night when I was hurting so badly from grief.

It was late June, and five months after Mark had crossed over. I was feeling so very sad. I had come home from work and was having a hard time adjusting to a life without Mark, my soul mate. I went to bed to try and take a nap, but mostly to escape the feeling of being so sad and lost.

My roommate had on the Country Music Television Station. Kellie Coffey was singing her new song "When You Lie Next to Me." I just closed my eyes and could feel the tears starting to stream down my face. With my eyes closed, I had a vision of Mark standing there right beside my bed. In my mind, I could see the look of love in his eyes. He leaned down and kissed me and then knelt down and just held me in his arms. But the ADC didn't end there. When I realized what all was going on in my mind's eye from this spiritual visit from Mark, I thought to myself, "Who can sleep now?"

I got up and went over to my computer and played one of the music cassette tapes Mark made of him playing his guitar. As I played tape, my computer started acting weird . . . it was going crazy, flashing off and on. It felt like I was getting a sign from Mark through the computer too! Eventually, I turned off the computer and I walked over to the sliding glass door to look outside. Out there on my chair was a big beautiful butterfly, just looking and staring back at me, slowly waving his wings back and forth. It was as if this butterfly had Mark's spirit inside of him and he was waving hello to me! The ADCs that Mark gave me on that memorable day, when I was hurting so badly, brought so much love and comfort to me. I am very thankful to Mark and to God for these blessings.

LAURA

Daddy's Back!

My dad was born and raised in Germany. He came to the U.S.A. in his twenties.

Daddy raised my sister Susie and me from the time we were three and four years old. I am the baby. He spoiled my sister and me rotten, and we loved it! When I was seven years old, he married my stepmom.

My son and I lived with my dad for four years before I married my current husband. During the time I lived with daddy, he helped to raise my son.

My dad's name is Eric. My son's name is David Eric. My sister named her daughter Erica. So my sister and I both named our babies after Dad!

After I married my husband and moved forty-five minutes away from the rest of the family, my sister Susie, Dad, and I would get together on Friday nights to have dinner at her house. Also, we always made a big deal out of Father's Day and Dad's birthday too. He never missed my or Susie's birthdays either. He was always there and bringing gifts.

Daddy was a mechanic by trade. I worked for Daddy at his garage, as his office manager, and my sister worked for him too. He was the kindest man. He never charged me for fixing my car. He would fix people's cars that didn't have much money and not charge them, and he did this all the time! When it came to older people, he would often undercharge them cause he knew they didn't have the money for the full rate! He also would give men jobs whom other people wouldn't give a chance.

My daddy was very well loved. He taught me how to love! He gave me so much love.

One night my dad was on his way home from work riding along a three-mile long bridge. A semi-tractor trailer lost its steering wheel and rode right on top of my dad's little Toyota car. This was on January 13, 1999.

I fell to my knees when my sister called and told me what had happened. That was the saddest day of my life. I could not breathe; my dad was like the air I breathed. I love him more than life.

Right after my daddy's funeral, my sister and I were sitting on the back porch, which is separated by sliding glass doors. We both looked in and saw my daddy plain as day sitting with his head down at the dining room table. We knew he had his head down because he was trying to show us that he knew we were so sad and missed him so very much.

We both could see him, yet he was semitransparent, so we were able to see through him, too. This vision lasted about a minute. We were sitting and gazing at our daddy one minute and then poof he was gone! We were both so amazed at this vision of our precious daddy.

This wonderful ADC only goes to show what I have always known in my heart, that my sister and my dad and I have a bond so strong, not even death can tear us apart

JACKIE & SUSIE

A Make Over by Barb

One day I was at Walmart going up and down the aisles, not really looking for anything in particular. All of a sudden I saw this very pretty lady up ahead of me. Instantly, I recognized her as Barb, a very dear and special friend with whom I immediately bonded when we first met and who crossed over on October 28, 2002. I said to myself, "Oh, there's

Barb!" completely forgetting in that moment in time, that she had passed. I quickened my pace keeping my eye on her, and before my eyes, she transformed into the woman she really was–not Barb at all! Actually the woman really bore no resemblance to Barb either.

Then I freaked out realizing what I had just witnessed firsthand–the transformation of this woman's features and stature before my very eyes. First she was Barb, and then she wasn't Barb! This gave me mixed emotions, delight at seeing Barb, and sorrow when reality set in and I understood that it was not Barb after all. However, that lady was Barb for a minute in Walmart, I am convinced of this. Shortly afterwards I felt a gentle breeze whisk by me and felt cool air down my neck, which I believed was Barb's spirit affirming her presence.

Later that same week, at approximately 11:15 p.m., I was on the computer but also had the psychic medium John Edward's Show on TV. He was talking about this lady who passed and her kids were trying to contact her. I looked up at the screen, and truthfully, the lady who the camera was on was Barb's face again. She looked exactly like she looks on her prayer card– beautiful with striking features, clear blue eyes, and with a smile that would light up any room. I watched intently, and within seconds, the woman also transformed completely from looking like Barb, again, into looking like a completely different face!

These two transformations, before my very eyes, concerning Barb's features in the same week, no less, were some of the most amazing experiences I have ever encountered in my life.

Now as if that were not enough, minutes after the John Edward episode, my cat and I were relaxing on the bed. I felt the bed go down as if someone had just sat down on it. This was not the first time that I have experienced this sensation, though. The cat apparently felt it too, as his eyes got like saucers and looked at me. I asked him if "Aunt Barb" was around? Well, he simultaneously began purring as if someone were stroking his silky white fur. I felt the bed go up as if someone were now getting off the bed. My cat stopped purring and then a thank you card that Barb had given to me in the past, which stands on my end table, fell off of the table. Of course, no one was near it, and there was no air coming from a fan or an open window.

I believe strongly it was yet another way for Barb to let me know she has not left me and she is still, and always will be, a very active part of my life even from Heaven.

KIM S. MANGAN

* * *

CHAPTER 26

Visions of Children

> Spiritual appearances from our children are heavenly treasures to soothe our aching hearts, until we can hug them again.

He Bit My Finger

I began my real spiritual journey after the death of my mom in 1995. Thank God I had, or I may not have made it after the loss of my son Scott in 1997, at the age of twenty-two.

In April 2000, my dad was diagnosed with terminal cancer. While hospitalized he was accidentally overdosed on a strong narcotic and was delirious for three days. Unfortunately, he never quite returned to his old self mentally. He suffered severe respiratory depression as a result of being overdosed. During those three days when he was delirious, he spoke many times to the spirits of my mom, my son, his parents and others who have passed. At one point he stated he would leave on the following Sunday at noon. He said he had to wait for Scottie, my son, who was busy just then in Heaven.

It was now Wednesday, and I brought him home believing he had at least two to three months left, but on Saturday morning he was in a coma. I called our family and my best friend Sue, who was like a daughter to my dad. She came immediately. We all waited with my dad through the day and into the evening. At 4 a.m. Sue went to lie down.

Sue and I never discussed the afterlife because we had agreed to disagree on this subject. I was a believer and Sue wasn't. However, Sue's view on the subject changed radically that morning. While lying down she said she felt like she was in a twilight sleep, although she could still hear us talking and moving around the house. Someone shook her on the shoulder. When she looked to see who it was, my son Scott was standing by the bed. He looked the same to Sue and his voice sounded the same to her from the last time she saw him.

He shook his finger at her and said, "You tell them I'm okay. You tell them I'm okay." He then picked up her hand and bit her finger— hard—she said it really hurt. He then said, "And don't you forget this!" Nothing else was said, and he then faded away. Sue felt he was there to help my dad make his transition. My dad died at 12:20 p.m. that Sunday, just like he said he would, and Scott had come for him, just like my dad said he would.

Scott definitely picked the right person to go to. He knew everyone would really know he had been there by going to a nonbeliever. While losing my dad was very difficult, knowing that my son helped him cross over and that they are all together, gave me a peace nothing else could.

PAM GRAY

I See You

Our son John B. Murtaugh passed at the young age of twenty-five from juvenile diabetes. The most validating type of ADC was received by my husband Kev and me to show that

John is in a new world—a dimension not even an arm's length away. I know this because Kev and I have both seen John in his spiritual body.

One day Kev was outside working in the yard and then walked over to his truck to get inside. As he sat in the driver's seat and was ready to drive off, he saw a shadow in the corner of his eye. He looked quickly, hoping he wasn't about to hit a child who was running. To his amazement, he saw our son John and yelled, "Whoa, John!" John stopped in front of his truck, turned to look at his dad, gave that special John-grin and left! Kev was so ecstatic that he jumped out of the truck and ran into the house to tell me what had just happened. From that day on, my husband has been at peace that John is more than just okay!

For me, it was about three weeks after John passed. The alarm clock went off. As I reached for it, I saw John by the side of the bed just looking at me! He wasn't sad or smiling, but just standing there, as if he were watching over me.

Also on another occasion, I received a visual message from John in my mind's eye. Night after night I would sit on the back patio late at night and watch this mist move in front of me. I would say, "Baby, I see you." I would put my hand into the mist to try and feel him. Well one morning, just after I awoke and was still lying in bed listening to my husband moving around and our bird chirping, I got a visual image in my mind's eye of a black box. Inside this box were white letters in italics and the words, "I SEE U." I knew then that John was with me when I was sitting on the patio. He was letting me know that he saw me too, by repeating the very words I said to him when I was on the patio!

What I've learned from my child, who left this world all too soon, is that there is no death—only life to life, and that he lives eternally, free of his disease and free to experience the wonders of the universe. While I can no longer hug my child as I used too, I know now that the Lord gives him my motherly hugs until someday when John holds his hand out to walk his mom Home.

CATHYJMF & KEV MURTAUGH

Mary Never Got a Day Older

Even though I am a prayerful person, I did not pray for this particular event to occur. I am a school crossing guard, stationed on the same road, for the last eight years. I cross kids three times a day—morning, lunch time and late afternoon. One day in the afternoon after all of the kids had safely crossed the road and I was just about to leave to go home, I saw another little girl coming down the road towards me. As she came near, I noticed that she looked different from the other kids. It was because of the way she was dressed. She was dressed the way little girls dressed back in the '40s!

Then I gasped. It could not be—it was Mary, my little playmate from childhood. I recognized her without her even having to identify herself. Regaining my composure, I said, "Hi," and she said, "Hello!" back. Her hair was black and in ringlets. I asked her who had done her hair. She said she did it herself. I next saw her mother's face form on the side of hers. Her mother looked to be around the age of twenty-five, even though her mother died at the age of eighty.

My little playmate died at the age of ten, some fifty-eight years ago, yet here she was as solid as me and even talking to me. She asked me, "Will you be here tomorrow?" I said, "Yes." With that she vanished and I never saw her again.

GEORGE STONE

CHAPTER 27

Pet Visitations

> Our pets and animals love us very much, as much as we love them. They, too, have a place in heaven with God. Their spirits can come back to visit us to provide comfort and to reassure us they are very, very happy!

Clink, Clink, Clink

Max, our golden retriever, had to be put down shortly after Thanksgiving. He was fourteen and truly a gentleman. Unusual description for a dog, but Max was special.

You need to know that Max slept on the floor on my side of the bed. Each morning he would begin his grooming, and he would make a very distinct noise while doing this. His grooming would cause his dog license to clink, and he would bang against my dresser causing the handle on the lower drawer to bang. The sound of his daily grooming was unlike any other sound in our house.

About a week after his passing, my husband and I were lying in bed, awake but quiet, each of us sobbing over the loss of our dear pet. It was very early and the world was still asleep and quiet—no sounds of traffic, birds, or life in general.

There we were quietly sobbing and thinking of our doggie when suddenly there was that same sound Max made each and every morning, and it seemed to be coming from the floor on my side of the bed! My husband and I both sat straight up in bed and leaned over to look, fully expecting to see Max there grooming and smiling.

There were no other inside or outside sounds, no wind, no earthquake (we lived in California at the time) no sonic booms, no other apparent cause for this sound. Hearing the old familiar "clink, clink, clink" at first startled us, and then brought a huge smile to our faces. Max was still around and he let us know that.

This special ADC occurred before the phenomena and term of ADCs were known to me. It's something my husband and I still talk about and will always remember.

PAT O.

My Pet Chicken

Our pets do visit us from the afterlife. Even pet chickens!

When I was 10 years old my uncle Normie gave us some live baby chicks for Easter, because his young son was not able to properly care for them. All but one of the chicks died. The one who lived became my personal pet. I took care of her, as I loved her and loved playing with her. (Although I didn't like having to clean up after her!)

My little chick grew into a very happy and playful hen. Because we lived in the city of Philadelphia and not on a farm or in a rural area, I used take her for walks around the concrete and asphalt neighborhood. So that she wouldn't run away and so no harm would befall her, I would tie a string type of a leash around her leg for our little walks.

When she died a little over six months later after she first came into my life, I was devastated. I watched her take her last gasping breaths, and I was so distraught that she couldn't be saved. She was my first loss in life.

My ADC: Fifty years later, I had a dream that I was walking on the beach with my pet chicken. I was a little concerned that she was going to wander off because she was running free, but she didn't.

I was asking people if they had some food that was healthy for a chicken to eat and someone gave me something for her. In the dream I was treating her like she was my little child. I had my arm around her and was helping her to eat and drink. It was such a warm and loving feeling being able to care for her once again. And then I woke up!

I couldn't believe that after all these years, God allowed me to get to be with my first and cherished pet—my little chicken. Our pets really do remember us and they do live on in Heaven.

CHRISTINE DUMINIAK

Pokey My Broodmare

Late March of 2017 I fed my large herd of horses, grateful for the long winter to be over and the sun to be out. It was going to be a nice warm spring day after a brutal cold and icy winter. I noticed my oldest broodmare Pokey laying on her side and thought she looked so comfortable, warming her old bones. Pokey was not struggling. Horses often lay on the sun-warmed ground to soak up the warmth.

Each spring I was grateful to see that she had survived one more of our long winters. Sadly, this time she would be the next to go from my band of aging broodmares

Later in the day when she was still laying down I knew she was in trouble. She looked like she could not get her feet out from under her in the mud; we hoped that we could get her up. My sister and I got a halter on her and pulled to give her something to balance on. She didn't even try to find her feet. We called a neighbor who brought his tractor over, and he tried to help pull her up. She made no effort, no struggle. We pulled her out of the mud in hopes that she was tired and just needed to rest, but I knew in my heart that she was headed Home. We covered her with horse blankets and offered her water. She was able to lift her head to drink. She ate grain and small handfuls of hay. She was not in any distress, not suffering at all, just unable to get to her feet. I thought that she had mostly likely suffered a stroke, and that she would surely not make it until the next morning.

She obviously was not ready to go. For eight days she lay on her side, not suffering, struggling or nickering for water and feed. So we made the decision to let her go peacefully on her own. A fellow horseman told me of horses that had recovered from strokes, and my sister and my friend, who were helping me with Pokey, wanted to give her every chance to recover. Euthanasia of a large animal with the huge heart of a horse is not always peaceful, so we wanted to avoid this if possible.

After eight days of laying on her side her eyes finally told me she was ready. For those eight long days someone was with her every few hours, offering her feed and water. We gave her supplements to aid with digestion and aspirin to make her comfortable. We lovingly groomed her long black mane and tail and her beautiful bay coat. I sat with her and remembered my dad buying her for me 24 years ago as a two-year-old. He surprised me with the gift of her on his annual visit to us at the ranch during our county fair. She was part of so many memories that included my dad and my husband Tom who died within one month of each other in 2010, and I was heartbroken to have to let her go. The vet came and agreed that she was ready and that her big ol' heart had kept her going when most horses would have given up. It was a peaceful end to a good long life.

Pokey had given me eight wonderful foals, one who became an AQHA World Champion. Her foals went on to enrich the lives of other horse lovers.

A week after we buried her on the ranch, I dreamed that we were out by the barn. There were four of us and I sensed that my late husband Tom was one of those people. Pokey appeared to us, youthful and strong, and indicated that she wanted all of us to get on her back. We were concerned that she could not carry four people, but she insisted—not in words, but with her eyes. We climbed on. I was in the front and holding onto her wonderful thick mane that I had so loved when she was with us. Tom was behind me with his arms around me, and my sister and my friend behind him. Pokey carried us through the pasture to the cottonwood trees lining the creek on the east side of the ranch, a place where we have buried many horses over the years. I call it the Ghost Herd.

I awoke from my dream in joy and peace at seeing my sweet girl, whole and sound, and knowing that my Tom was there with her. I can't say I consciously asked for a dream visit from her, but my heart was always open to the possibility. I often dream of my horses. My dad once asked me if I did, and I said "Yes. They talk to me in my dreams and sometimes I run with them. They have the most beautiful voices." He said, "I knew that." I can't tell you how much peace the dream brought me and my sister and friend. It brought us all so much joy.

CLAUDIA

My Cat And Her Rocking Chair

I lost my beloved cat Taz very suddenly on December 14, 2001. He was almost four years old at the time. He had a bladder blockage that, sadly, I was unaware of. He was big, black, furry, and so beautiful. He was always there for me when I was in emotional pain, and I always felt like he was my guardian. I used to tease and say that Taz was my guard cat. Taz especially brought me great comfort after the loss of my infant daughter in April 2001. She was born prematurely and only lived for one hour.

One of Taz's favorite places to sit and nap was on my rocking chair. He used to lie on the back of it, and the rocking chair would rock back and forth every time. Taz would jump up on it just to rest awhile.

Following Taz's death, my oldest son and I had a few dreams of Taz. In these dreams he appeared beautiful and in perfect health, and he always had a glow of white light radiating around him. These dreams always left me with a sense of peace and comfort.

After the last dream visit I had from Taz, I was walking into my living room and the empty rocking chair, where Taz used to nap, started rocking very swiftly of its own accord. It so reminded me of the times when Taz used to jump on it to rest. I knew when I saw that rocking chair rock by itself, with no one around it, my dear beloved Taz was there in his spiritual body and was letting me know he was still with me.

TRACI

My Cockatiel Teeko

The evening of April 29, 2006 I came back from a successful seminar I held in New York City with a song in my heart. However, as soon as I entered my house I was immediately hit with the devastating news from my husband that my beloved cockatiel named Teeko accidentally had flown out the door earlier in the day.

It seems that the delivery men who had come to our house to deliver a new sofa, had left our front door wide open before my husband had a chance to get Teeko back into his cage. Teeko flew right out the door and out of our lives.

I really loved this little bird who I had adopted from a pet store many years earlier, and I was heartbroken. But I didn't give up on him. I frantically searched the neighborhood and was able to finally locate him the next day.

He was living high up in a tree a block away from our house in our same development. Some really kind neighbors Jack and his wife Connie whose tree Teeko was hanging out in, and to whom I was a perfect stranger, let me stay on their patio deck for 8 hours, as I tried to coax Teeko down out of that tree. Teeko had a distinctive whistle that sounded like the Woody the Woodpecker whistle, so I repeatedly used his special whistle trying to call him down to me and back into his cage. I did this for two days. Unfortunately, Teeko was too afraid to come down and he was too high up to be reached. Sadly, by the thrid day he was gone. I hung many fliers around town, checked animal and bird shelters, internet bird sites, and drove from street to street looking for him, but to no avail. I found myself crying every night and praying to God for little Teeko, as I was so worried about his safety and welfare.

Finally, a few weeks later I contacted my guardian angel through my dear friend the Christian medium, Sunni Welles. I asked my angel what he knew about Teeko. My angel shared that eventually two children had found Teeko in a park, and that he was living in a good home. I was greatly relieved to hear this news. I was also blessed to have been given another cockatiel from my next door neighbor the same day Teeko flew away. Even though he wasn't my Teeko, he was a good diversion through my grief and sorrow.

Nine months had gone by since Teeko flew out of our lives. One morning I was lying in bed and was shown a vision of these significant words, "Don't grieve for me" written on a fancy scroll banner. There were birds all around this banner. I wanted to know for sure who this message was from, so I asked for Jesus' protection, and then I asked out loud who was this poem from? To my amazement and delight I was shown a cockatiel!

I realized that I was being told that the comforting words were from Teeko and that he was now safely in Heaven. At first I started to cry because I realized he had died. Then I remembered "Duh, he is in Heaven, what better place could there be for him!" Even though I had greatly missed my little Teeko, my main concern was that he was safe. What could be safer than being with God in Heaven?

The next 2 nights after that vision I had a dream in which I was with a cockatiel, and I was demonstrating to people on how to hold a bird so that he doesn't fly away! I believe these dreams were more validations about Teeko who was in Heaven and who came to spend a little time with me in my dream state. He wanted me to know that he was great, and OK and still around me! Truly these visits were a healing balm to my grieving heart and soul.

CHRISTINE DUMINIAK

Shadow & Bogart

Our dear Lhasa Apso passed. We then wanted another dear fur baby but a different breed, so he wouldn't be a painful reminder. Our choice was a Shih Tzu. I have had dear dogs all my life, but I had an experience that I never dreamt would happen to me. What dear souls they are.

We named our Shih Tzu Bogart because to us he looked just like Humphrey Bogart. I loved him dearly. We then got another dog to keep him company, named Shadow. The three of us were always together at the park, shopping, etc.

Bogart eventually developed diabetes. He became very ill very suddenly. I couldn't reach his vet and finally got hold of a clinic. I was on my way over there, but dear Bogart passed before we arrived in time for help. It was November 24, 1994, at 3:40 a.m. It was completely unexpected. Shadow whined, howled, and yes, there were tears; he, too, cried.

One evening when I was holding Shadow, I saw Bogart walk across the room. He came over, sat at my feet, looked up at me, and said telepathically to me, "I'm fine, take care of Shadow. He needs you." I reached for him but he was gone. I knew then he was okay, and I was astounded by this visit.

I thought about what Bogart said, and he was right, Shadow did need me. I lived alone with my fur babies for seven years, as my husband and I had divorced. My children had moved out to start their own families. Shadow and I spent all the holidays together.

I always loved Christmas Eve the most. It was so serene. I would wrap some presents for Shadow too. We would open our gifts on Christmas morning and Shadow would get so excited about all the gifts too. I would get something from him to me. It was a lot of fun.

I loved Shadow like he was my baby. I would ride him in a stroller to the park three times a day. Shadow seemed to really enjoy the stroller rides and all the attention that came with it.

Eventually, Shadow developed a blood disorder. He couldn't make red blood cells, and the vet didn't know why. He was on many medications to help him, but Shadow lost weight, and he couldn't eat or drink the last four days of his life. He didn't give up and didn't want to surrender his life. He seemed like he wanted to get better, even though he was suffering so. He was in so much pain. I never had to make a life-or-death choice before, but I did not want to see Shadow suffer any longer, so I made the decision to have the vet put him to sleep, in order to end his suffering. This was on October 10, 2000.

I still have deep guilt over this. I was grieving so very badly and I prayed for a sign that Shadow was okay and with Bogart. I prayed and was sitting on my bed crying my eyes out when I felt a calm come over me. I looked at the ceiling above me and saw what now looked like the sky. It had a pink background, and then from a distance I saw a huge bouquet of the largest pink roses. Also in the distance I saw two figures that appeared like clouds of energy. Both the roses and these clouds of energy floated right up near me. The clouds of energy were chasing and touching each other. It reminded me of how Bogart and Shadow looked when they played together, hiding and chasing each other behind the roses.

I knew it was their way of telling me they were together having fun and that they loved me and would be there for me when it was my turn to join them.

I never thought of the afterlife or praying until after my dear, sweet, precious Shadow passed. Now I pray every day. I found my way back to God because of these two precious souls. I'm praying to see and to talk to them again, but most of all I need to hold them and tell them how much I love them. I can feel Shadow and Bogart close to me. Our love is there for each other through all eternity.

KATHY F.

Buttons

We prayed to find the right puppy for our family, and God led us to a precious good-natured pup, who fit in so perfectly with our family. We just loved our newest little addition, a white cock-a-poo who we named Sandy.

Because our little Sandy had yet to be house broken, we thought it best for now to have her sleep in her cage in the kitchen at night. One night I was lying in bed and I saw a small white dog on our bed, lying between my husband and me. I thought to myself, "Why is Sandy in bed with us? I thought she was in her cage in the kitchen." Then I saw this white dog float towards the ceiling and disappear!

I wondered what the heck was going on, so I went out to the kitchen to see where Sandy was. But Sandy was still locked in her cage! I was bewildered. Then it dawned on me. Years ago my mom and dad had a small white poodle, named Buttons. We all loved her. Buttons lived to be sixteen years old and my heartbroken dad had to have Buttons put to sleep, because she was suffering from so many health problems. Even though this broke his heart, he felt this was the kindest thing to do for her.

I realized that Buttons had come back to visit us (after being in Heaven for sixteen years) to let us know she is still with our family, as she lives on happily with God. It wouldn't surprise me if Buttons was going to be around to play with Sandy from time to time. This visit from Buttons would later prove to be even more meaningful after my dad got called back

Home four months later. I knew he and his precious Buttons were together again and having a ball playing together just like in the good old days!

CHRISTINE DUMINIAK

My Dog—Nurse Goldie

Goldie was our family dog. She was the kindest creature in the world. We know she was sent to us from God because her first owner died from cancer, and then my dad inherited her.

At first when the owner had wanted to will Goldie to my father, my mother said, "No," but my dad knew my mother would love Goldie, so he agreed to take her at the appropriate time. Goldie seemed to be blessed with a mature, old soul. She came to live with us when I was about five years old, and she passed when I was a young woman. Our family cried, and my mother was especially sick with grief. Mom would say that she knew all dogs were sent from God because they are so loyal and loving. They love unconditionally.

One time after her passing, Goldie came to visit me in my dreams. I had been very sick with the flu at the time. I could not leave my bed because I didn't have enough energy. In this dream visit I saw Goldie sitting at the top of the steps as she always did. She sat there and I could read her thoughts. She was with me because I was sick and she was watching over me.

When I woke, I knew that in addition to human angels, we also have pet angels to whom God gives individual souls. Since they are of love, then they are of God. I now know that when ever I am sick, our family dog Goldie never leaves my side.

God is an awesome God to assign a little soul and spirit to a dog. It is comforting to know that animals live forever too!

NATELY

The Bridge Kids' Memory Wall

I often remember and honor my two dear, sweet fur kids by lighting candles for them. I always feel so close to them when I light candles for them, and it helps my missing them so very much. One was with me for seventeen years and the other for twelve of those years. My fur kids were truly family and took part of my heart with them when they went back Home to God. I miss my two sweet ones, like others miss their children.

On Monday nights there is a service for pets on the Internet at The Bridge Kids' Memory Wall. I will pull up the names on my computer screen of the other pets that are on the Memory Wall list, and I remember them by lighting candles for them too.

Every so often this deep sorrow and loneliness comes back, so I had been praying to God. I asked Him to please allow my one fur kid in particular to visit me, no matter how short it might be, as I really needed to see him.

My prayers were answered one night after I had lit candles to honor my two dear fur kids. I was sitting in my living room, watching the candles glow. I was missing them and thinking about them. I suddenly noticed in the reflection of my eyeglasses that I could see my sweet fur kids. They showed themselves to me one at a time and they repeated this a few times, always taking turns. I felt as if I could just reach over and pick them up.

One stretched and held his little head up just the way he did when he smelled something yummy. It was so real. His dear eyes were as bright and alive as they were when he was young, not as they were when he passed—he was blind then.

Then a few other animals further surprised me by their spiritual appearances too. One dog was a pug, who I recognized as the one I had as a child. A white cat also came; next a larger brown-and-white dog. Then towards the end of this amazing visit, many dogs came together as a group.

I believe these were some of the pets who I have remembered and lit candles for from The Bridge Kids' Memory Wall. I believe they were thanking me by making a visual appearance to me. I thanked them all for coming. I told my two sweet fur kids how happy it made me to see them together again and to please come back soon. I just can't believe how natural it all seemed. It was like they were home here again. I am so thankful and so very grateful to God for these visits.

SCOOTER

* * *

CHAPTER 28

Warnings & Premonitions

Heavenly intervention played a key role in these warnings and premonitions.

My Soul Agreement With Aly

One night in 2007, I had a vivid dream. I was the front passenger in a car and my teen daughter Aly was sitting behind the driver. Suddenly, the car missed a curve in the road and sailed into a lake. The driver and I escaped the sinking car, but Aly did not. As I bobbed to the surface, I dove again and again in the murky water desperately searching for my daughter. But I failed to find her. My beloved daughter was gone, leaving behind nothing other an open book floating on the water in the spot where she disappeared.

Two years later, on August 5, 2009, that horrible nightmare became a reality when Aly died as a backseat passenger in a car accident.

Returning home from a swim meet, the car carrying Aly and two of her teammates was T-boned by a father coming home from work. My beautiful fifteen-year-old daughter took the brunt of the impact, and died instantly. She was the only fatality.

Against the odds—and surely due to divine intervention—I came upon the scene of the accident. The high-speed impact sent both vehicles flying into a farmer's field. I made my way through the tall grass toward the twisted wreckage like a wild animal searching for her young. I found her on the ground next to the rear passenger door. My precious baby girl with the smooth tanned skin and long blonde hair, the strong broad swim shoulders and tiny waist, my stellar student with fierce determination and dedication to reach the Olympics, was strapped to a backboard and draped by a stark white sheet. I knelt down beside her and searched for her hand under the sheet's edge. I sat in the grass and held her soft hand in mine, too shocked to cry.

Behind me stood a large group of emergency responders and law enforcement officers, hushed respectfully as they took in the scene. I could feel the collection of raw, powerful compassion. And then for no particular reason, I looked up into the dark field that stretched before us, and that is when I saw my daughter with my beloved grandmother, who had died thirteen years prior. She had an arm around Aly and was gently leading her away. Aly was looking over her shoulder at me as she walked beside the great-grandmother she never knew. Walking away from me, forever.

Seeing the world through a filter of sorrow, I found comfort by helping others who were struggling. This fueled my passion to create a legacy of help, healing and hope. I founded AlyBlue Media in 2013 and launched Grief Diaries Radio in February 2014. I soon added film, webinars, and books to my repertoire as well as national events including the National Grief & Hope Convention featuring Martin Luther King's daughter, Dr. Bernice King. I was so moved by all the stories that were swapped that weekend at the Convention that I decided to invite grievers to share them in a book series called

Grief Diaries. Over a hundred people in six countries registered as contributors and the first eight books were published in December 2015. Now home to more than 600 writers spanning the globe, Grief Diaries has 25 titles in print with more on the way.

Because of that floating book my daughter left behind in my dream premonition, I now understand that the dream I had in 2007 was actually a glimpse into a Divine plan destined to bring comfort, healing and hope to people around the world through sharing stories in the Grief Diaries.

Not only does it help both reader and writer, but the written words has become a portable support group for those who share the same path. It's comforting to know someone else understands the shoes we walk in, and the challenges we face along the way. Although no two journeys are identical, the Grief Diaries stories are proof that none of us are truly alone. For we walk ahead, behind, and right beside you.

LYNDA CHELDELIN FELL
Creator of award-winning Grief Diaries book series
www.griefdiaries.com

Back Out Of It Now!

On a Saturday morning, around 11:45 a.m., I was driving to pick up my son from a friend's house. I got the strangest sensation to avoid getting on the expressway. However, because traffic was very heavy on the side streets, I decided to travel on the expressway, anyway, despite this nagging feeling.

As I continued on my journey on the expressway, I was nearing an exit where I could get off to take side streets the rest of the way to reach my destination, but I made the mental decision to continue on the expressway anyway, thinking it would get me there faster. At the exact moment that I made the decision to stay on the expressway, these words were involuntarily blurted out of my mouth, "BACK OUT OF IT, NOW!"

Please understand this was not my female voice but that of a male's voice speaking out of my mouth! This paranormal occurrence scared me terribly, yet immediately with no conscious effort on my part, I obediently began to go towards the exit.

Just as I was beginning my exit onto the off ramp, a large RV, carrying bicycles and a car, began to spin uncontrollably right in front of my small car. As I was exiting off to the side, the bicycles began flying through the air. I looked in my side view mirror, and I saw cars being struck by the bikes as the RV crashed into other cars. I was so frightened that I had to pull off to the side of the road and park to regain my composure, not only from the accident that barely missed me, but also from the episode of having a male's voice speak out of my mouth!

Nothing like this has ever happened to me before. I now realize that I had Divine intervention that day in that moment in time. God reached me in a way that would get my undivided attention in order to save me from certain disaster.

LINDA

Always With Us

On August 4, 1999, my grandfather passed away. I come from a very large family and he had always told me that I was his favorite grandchild. His death was very upsetting because he was only sixty-three years old and I loved him so.

After my grandfather passed away, my family and I were staying with my grandmother to comfort her and to be sure that she wouldn't be in the house alone. One night there were quite a few people staying with her, so my parents insisted that I go back home. It was late and my grandparents' house is not in a safe neighborhood. So against the will of my parents I stayed at my grandparents' house anyway.

Just as everyone settled in for bed, I went over to a picture of my grandfather where my grandmother had set up a burning candle on each side of the picture. I gently blew out both candles and went to sleep on the couch in the same room.

Around 4 a.m. my car alarm went off, and I was terrified. I peeked out the window and saw a man in a white T-shirt sitting in my car with the door open. I immediately called 911 and woke everyone up. We all carefully peeked through the window and saw what appeared to be a robber. Later, the police arrived and I went outside with them to see the damage that was done to my car. As I approached my vehicle, I noticed that it was completely untouched. The policeman told me that they would take fingerprints, but the dew on the door handle looked as if it hadn't even been touched! They told me it was probably my imagination, although my imagination did not make the car alarm go off. Plus, I had witnesses with me who also saw there was someone sitting inside my car!

After the police left, I decided that there was nothing more for me to do but to go on back to sleep. I went back and laid on the couch facing the wall. Still feeling anxious, I turned over onto my other side and suddenly noticed that the candles, which I had blown out hours ago, were lit again! I could tell they had been burning only for a short time. I questioned everyone in the house, and no one had lit those candles!

I still have the police report even today. I am not exactly sure how to interpret this experience, but I will never forget it. Maybe my grandfather protected me from the robber, or just wanted to prove to us that he would still be with us and we could feel secure. Certainly, in my eyes, this was an unbelievable experience.

ROMEA MIRZANIKOLAY

The Jangling Keys

I lost my sweetheart Honey (Jim) at the age of fifty-three. Two weeks later I believe he was there with me to protect me. I live in a townhouse and it was always Honey's job to make certain that the front door was locked before we went to sleep. I would constantly forget as I relied on Honey to do so. A month or so before Honey's final hospitalization, I began sleeping on the couch in the living room. I didn't want to disturb Honey's sleep and thought it was better if I just camped out on the couch.

About a week after Honey's funeral, I was asleep on the couch and the jangling of the front door keys that always remain in the deadbolt lock awakened me. The front door is probably three feet from where my head was. My eyes shot open and I was expecting someone to come into the house. No one was there (thank goodness), and then I remembered I had forgotten to lock the door before I went to sleep. I thanked Honey for making sure I was safe and I got up to lock the door!

JO LYNN

The Creaking Floorboards

I was home alone and getting dressed to go to work when I heard creaking floorboards overhead. The noise sounded like a man's heavy footsteps walking across the floor of my son's bedroom directly above me. I wondered how that could be because I was home alone. Or so I thought!

I checked the front and rear doors and found that they were still locked. I then proceeded to slowly and cautiously creep up the stairs to check out those heavy-sounding footsteps. When I opened the door to my son's bedroom, I found myself staring at an empty room; however, his electrical ceiling fan was left on and spinning. Since we had a small but potentially serious fire in the past, I am extremely conscious of electrical malfunctions being a fire hazard. I am forever reminding the kids to turn off all electrical devices in their rooms before they go out.

As I stood there by myself in his empty bedroom, staring at the spinning ceiling fan, I realized that the creaking floorboards, made by an invisible protector, were meant to get my attention, so I would go upstairs to investigate. My protector wanted to be sure that I attended to that spinning ceiling fan before I went out for the day.

I had this strong sense that my protector was my dear father-in-law John, the one who bought that ceiling fan for our son, a few years before John was called Home by God. Thank you, dear John, and thank You, dear Jesus.

CHRISTINE DUMINIAK

Don't Swerve

My son Tommy had been killed in a work-related accident. This was two years prior to a particular day in February, when I was given a dire warning from Heaven.

I had driven Tommy's five-year-old daughter, my dear granddaughter, to her cousin's birthday party in a town one hour away. The road is a two-lane, paved country road with not much traffic and with critters sometimes crossing the road, which you always have to be on the lookout for.

On this particular day in February, there was no snow on the road, although the adjoining fields were blanketed in snow. I have driven this road hundreds of times for over twenty-five years in all kinds of weather, and it does not make me nervous, for I know this road very well.

It was now close to 8 p.m. and the birthday party was ending. We were getting ready to leave to begin our one-hour drive to return home. It was a dark, moonless, and clear night, and for some unexplained reason I started getting a feeling of anxiety and butterflies in my stomach.

I was very nervous as we drove away to begin our journey home. The feeling was so strong that I seriously considered turning around and going back. The feeling became more intense as we drove farther along. My granddaughter had fallen asleep in the front seat beside me. I kept watching her and thinking she should be in the back seat. Then I heard a voice mumble, "If something is on the road, DON'T SWERVE!"

I am not sure if the first word I heard was "Mum" or not, but now I knew the reason for my feelings of anxiety. I calmed down but still nervously watched the road ahead, all the while carrying on an internal conversation in my mind with my son, asking why he didn't remove the problem before we got there?

A cat ran across the road and I wondered if this was what I was being warned about. But the sensation of fear was still with me. By now it had been a thirty-minute nerve-wracking drive and we were still thirty minutes away from home. We came up a small rise and suddenly in front of me was the biggest, slowest raccoon I have ever seen. Unfortunately, it was in the path of my van, but following the voice's advice, I did not swerve. That particular place on the road has deep ditches on each side and very little traffic. We could have easily ended up badly hurt in the deep ditch, hurt and stranded.

Now I am an avid animal lover and my usual instinct would have been to avoid any little beasts on the road, even frogs! Although I was feeling very sad to have killed this innocent creature, I now realized the anxiety had disappeared and calm came over me. My internalized conversation turned to grateful thanks and love for the warning. I do believe my son warned me and prevented his daughter and me from being injured or worse.

EILEEN MOORBY

* * *

AFTER-DEATH COMMUNICATIONS

* * *

PART III
Healing From Grief

CHAPTER 29

Why Do Bad Things Happen To Good People?

Your Soul Agreement

There is an age-old question that most people grapple with and that is, Why do bad things happen to good people? So many good and wonderful adults and innocent children, who we personally know, hear or read about, seem to be unfairly targeted for horrific sufferings they endure on earth. The fact that some die, way before their time, can strike us as being shockingly heartless and cruel. Why would a loving Creator allow us to suffer or die in such dreadful ways? Why wouldn't He step in to stop it?

Answer: Soul agreements.

It may surprise you to learn that we humans were all created spirits in Heaven by God *before* we came down to earth to live in a physical body. Every spirit makes a personal soul agreement with God in Heaven about what they want to experience on earth. These soul agreements were made for the purpose of advancing our soul's spiritual growth, (as well as others who are connected to us in our lives). Why? In order to get closer to God and to reach higher spiritual realms when we return to Heaven. Many will find it a shock to learn that we actually *volunteer* for the great hardships and challenges we endure on earth, as well as how we are going to die.

Suffering and hardships from diseases, disabilities, accidents and natural disasters are but a few of the hundreds of adversities that we humans go through, that have been agreed upon and volunteered in advance by one's own soul. God doesn't force anything on us. He does, however, allow us to view in advance the rough blueprints of our lives, and what the soul's tremendous spiritual growth will be by choosing and successfully completing our challenges.

You may wonder who in the world would sign up for these sufferings? What *were* they thinking? When the spirit-soul views these challenges and their deaths in advance in Heaven, they view it from the standpoint of objectivity and not subjectively. Therefore, at the time that these challenges were chosen in Heaven, they seemed very doable. They also know that God will give them all the spiritual assistance and strength they need, if they pray to God to help them. This is why spirits are so courageous in choosing their lessons, goals and missions.

Although the soul could stay in Heaven forever instead, where life is easy and perfect, spirits would only be able to grow at a very slow rate to advance to higher spiritual realms and closer to God. Because spirits are very desirous to grow at a fast rate, is why they are eager to come to earth where life is hard to successfully overcome great obstacles.

Every detail of our lives on earth are not set in stone, however. In Heaven, spirit-souls get to view the intended rough blueprint of their lives. We are also given free will to fill in the chapters of our lives by the choices we make on earth.

When we are born into our physical bodies here on earth, our spirit-souls' prior agreements about our chosen paths are erased from our memories. The good news is that our soul agreement memories are fully restored when our earthly physical lives are finished. We can then review our life's earthly accomplishments and the ripple effect that our choices and actions have impacted on ourselves and others. For instance, if we chose to have Lou Gehrig's Disease, cancer, MS, COPD, heart disease, cystic fibrosis, cerebral palsy, war injuries, to name a few, it may be more than just being about digging deep within to find the courage and strength to go through it. It may also be about giving others in our lives (known as our Soul Group Families) the opportunity to bring out the very best side of them to help in their souls' growth, too.

Premonitions—We can actually receive premonitions of disastrous future events to come in our lives. God sometimes gives us these premonitions to help prepare us for the event, as well as to validate that the event was part of our soul group agreement. To assure us that nothing we could have done would have changed the eventual outcome. As an example of this, please read the story in this book called "My Soul Agreement With Aly" in Chapter 28, Warnings & Premonitions, page 225. In that heart-wrenching true story a mother was given a frightening dream premonition of her teenage daughter Aly's death due to a car accident. This dream occurred two years prior to Aly's actual death from an auto accident. In that dream the mother was shown how her daughter's death was going to be the catalyst for her to eventually become an author. Over the years the mother has become a prolific writer, publisher, and international advocate for the bereaved. This was a predetermined soul agreement pact between the mother and daughter made in Heaven with God for a much greater good for the world.

Reincarnation—Some have asked me about the concept of reincarnation. Although this is an interesting concept that many people enjoy exploring and believe in, it really doesn't matter whether or not you believe in reincarnation. What does matter though is how you live your precious gift of life in *this* lifetime. So try to do your very best to make the most of your time here and now on earth.

Straying From Your Soul Agreement

Everyone has been given a free will by God to make their own choices on earth to either grow closer to God or to move away from Him. Those who stray from the rough blueprint of their life's path, e.g. through the choice of substance abuse, traveling with the wrong crowd, living recklessly, etc. can actually incur much more in the way of heartache, suffering, setbacks and even an earlier death than they had originally signed up for.

Destructive temptations are everywhere. That is why it is essential that one stays close to God when living an earthly experience. Praying to God can assist tremendously in staying on track by strengthening the spirit against harmful physical temptations. Praying brings God directly into your life and He will send you more angelic support, strength, and the right people to assist you—if you ask. Praying to God can also lessen one's physical and emotional pain. That is how powerful praying to God can be.

Choosing One's Death

As well as every spirit volunteering for their life lessons and missions in this school of earth, most spirits know how they are actually going to die. This too is part of their soul agreement with God. For example those who die of war wounds, terrorist attacks, accidents, murder, diseases, natural disasters, etc. have chosen how they are going to "go out" as part of their soul agreement.

In the case of children who die young (e.g. SIDS, diseases, illnesses, etc.) they are often Angels Unawares. Meaning that they had pure souls of angels who courageously volunteered to come to earth and die early to bring about a greater spiritual good for their families and humankind. Adults can also be Angels Unawares. You can read more about Angels Unawares in the enlightening spiritual book, *Glimpses of Heaven From the Angels Who Live There* by Sunni Welles.

It is also very possible to stray from our chosen paths, and die earlier or in a different way than was originally planned, if we don't stay close to God.

Survivors Guilt

Why me? If you were spared death when your buddies, family, neighbors, associates, buddies, and others around you were not (e.g. through war, terrorists attacks, accidents, fires, natural disasters, contagions, murder, etc.), that is because your mission on earth has not yet been completed. You have more work to do.

Have you ever heard of people who have had a near-death experience and found themselves traveling toward the Light, but were told to go back, because it was not yet their time? Well, even though you may not have had that wondrous supernatural experience of traveling towards the Light, it was not yet your time either! That is why you were spared.

The others, who were called Home while you were left behind, had most likely completed their missions and life lessons. They were being called Home for their heavenly rewards. Contrary to popular human belief, children or adults who have died, or whose lives were cut short, were not being punished, unlucky, or gypped out of living a long life by a heartless, uncaring God. Remember, these souls actually volunteered and signed up with God for how they were going to die. So God was faithfully fulfilling His part of their spiritual contract.

Those souls who were taken, while you were spared, are being given a glorious life full of unconditional love with God. They actually now get to talk and pray to God in person. They pray to God on your behalf too.

They are out of pain, at peace, able to fly by their thoughts, young again, and living in Paradise. They have reunited with their loved ones and pets. In Heaven there are loving, peaceful animals, mountains, valleys, lakes, oceans, gorgeous sunsets, beautiful flowers and gardens. There are majestic buildings, libraries of knowledge, lovely dwelling places and prayer centers. They can play musical instruments, participate in sports, dancing, do gardening, cook, read books, and have actual service jobs in Heaven. They continually get to explore Heaven and learn from angels and accomplished spirits. There is a spiritual realm for everything. Yet, they still get to see and hear their loved ones from the heavenly realms!

(For more descriptive insights into Heaven, please read *Embraced by the Light* by Betty Eadie. Betty Eadie had an amazing and comprehensive near-death experience, where she was taken all around Heaven and was sent back to earth to share her wondrous insights.)

If you were to talk to your friend or loved one who has passed, they would ask to you to be happy for them, not sad, because they are out of harm's way now and are "living the dream" in Heaven! They would assure you that they are not missing out on anything—because they can do and have everything in Heaven that we can do here on earth—and much, much more.

Dying is *not* a tragedy for the one whose spirit-soul releases from their physical body to return Home. It is a rite of passage, a completion of the circle of life (Heaven-Earth-Heaven) that we are all striving for, and a wonderful relief. A time of joy, awe and celebration for those who are back Home with their loving Creator.

They would want you to know that their death was also meant to be a gift to you to help you in your own soul's spiritual growth. That the ripple effect of their death, and your surviving, was meant to spur you in a certain direction to fulfill your own destiny, and perhaps for you to eventually bring comfort to others. Their death and your not dying, more than likely was an actual spiritual pact you made together in Heaven. For instance if your buddy, child, father, mother, husband, brother or sister died in a war, your part of the spiritual pact might be to one day help other Gold Star Families, wounded warriors, or homeless veterans in some way. Your loved ones' death was meant to bring about a greater good for you too.

I want to reiterate what I wrote under the heading Soul Agreements above and how receiving premonitions can help us to accept disastrous events to come in our lives. God sometimes gives us these premonitions to prepare us for the event, as well as to validate that the event was part of our soul group agreement, and nothing we could have done would have changed the outcome. As an example of this, please read the heart-wrenching and powerful story in this book called "My Soul Agreement With Aly" in Warnings & Premonitions in Chapter 28, page 255.

Your loved ones would also want you to know this is only a temporary separation. That they will reunite with you in Heaven, when it is your time to come Home. In the meantime they are helping you here on earth to successfully complete your own special mission. Not only are they with you in their spiritual bodies, they are more than likely giving you after-death signs and dream visitations of their presence around you. They can still see and hear you and will try to let you know this by the afterlife signs they are giving. Spirits in Heaven can be in more than one place at a time. They have supernatural powers now, so that is why this is possible with God's permission.

If you were spared death when others around you were not, then God wants you to realize that it was not yet your time to bring you Home for your rewards. Why? Because you still have a very important mission and work to do, to help others, and for lessons still to be learned on earth. Sometimes there may even be a Divine Intervention for how you were spared, if it is "not yet your time." Please realize how important your life on earth is to your soul's growth and to others around you. Please don't waste precious moments by being held captive to unnecessary guilt. Guilt will only hold you back from fulfilling your important reason for being here. Guilt can plunge you into deep despair and even suicide, thus robbing you of fulfilling the very reason why God sent you to earth and why you wanted to come. God will help you get over the guilt you may be feeling, and to help you find your purpose in life, if you ask Him. If you understand and accept that each soul has made an agreement with God, it will be much easier for you to let go of the guilt. Everything happens for a spiritual reason. God will turn everything around for good in the end. You may not understand the reasons now, but someday it will be revealed to you.

Try to find your purpose in life, so that when you are called Home, you can view your life's review in front of God with pride of accomplishment! At the time of your life's review, you will see how the people you interacted with on earth were actually buddies/soul group family members all meant to help one another's spiritual growth.

Please reinvest in life because your life is a priceless gift from God. Don't waste it. You have much more work to do! Your life matters to many, many people. You are an important and integral piece of the puzzle in numerous people's lives. There is a ripple effect to everyone whose lives you have touched and will touch. Please seek out the spiritual, emotional, mental, and physical help you need to reinvest in life.

Remember that each and every one of us signs up with God for how we are going to return back Home. It is always about the soul's agreement with God. You are not God and you do not have the ability to change anyone's spiritual agreement with God, no matter how much you wish you could or think you are responsible. That is why you must let go of your unnecessary guilt, my dear friend. It is out of your hands. God is the Giver and Taker of life.

Suicides and the Power of Prayers

Are You Thinking About Suicide?

If you or anyone you know is feeling suicidal, it is crucial to seek out help. God does not want us to take our own lives. He wants us to use our precious gift of life as an opportunity to successfully complete our lessons, earthly missions for important soul growth and to become closer to Him. If you are feeling suicidal, please get the spiritual, emotional, mental, physical, and medical help you need as soon as possible. The National Suicide Prevention Hotline is 1-800-273-8255. In the Resources section of this book, there is more information for veterans.

Many people have found a healing and healthy outlet for depressing and crippling thoughts by channeling their emotions through volunteering, writing, music and creative arts. There is a special bond that can form with people who have gone through similar traumas. Seeking out groups with participants who have been similarly impacted, can give enormous support. For instance, Veterans who are suffering from PTSD, and may be contemplating suicide, have received help through volunteer veterans groups, such as Warrior Songs. Here they experience camaraderie with other vets—perhaps the only other people who understand what they went through, while using art and music to process their feelings.

Writing can greatly help to express one's inner feelings and turmoil. If your suicidal thoughts are because of the inconsolable grief you are feeling over a lost loved one, please write the loved one or buddy a letter, expressing your emotions to them. Read your letter out loud to them with a photo of them smiling in front of you. Our loved ones in Heaven continue to see and hear us. Your letter will bring them to you. Ask God to bless you with an afterlife contact from your loved one, so you will recognize that they are still a huge part of your life and can still see and hear you.

Ask your clergy and others to pray for you. Prayers are so powerful. Even though you may be contemplating suicide as an escape from crippling pain and suffering, please remember there will be a devastating ripple of grief, pain, loss, shock, suffering and guilt to those who you will leave behind who love and care about you. Their pain and guilt can last a lifetime.

Are You Grieving A Suicide?

For those of you who do know of someone who has taken their own life, and they had a brain chemical imbalance, God knows better than anyone what their circumstances were. If your loved one was afflicted with mental illness, and has chosen to take their own life because of it, God does not hold that person responsible for his or her actions. God understands and is always merciful, even to those suicides who did not have a brain chemical imbalance. It is actually the soul who is regretful if they cut their life shorter than was planned. But again never doubt God's unconditional love, understanding, and mercy for each and every soul. We are all His "kids."

Our fervent prayers are very powerful. If you are concerned about your loved one or their soul, because of a suicide or perhaps the destructive type of life they may have lived, please pray for them. Your prayers on their behalf will help them tremendously to forgive themselves before God (if they have not yet already done so). Your prayers will help them to move on to higher spiritual realms. Your loved ones sincerely appreciate your prayers and are very, very grateful for them. They may even find a way to say thank you in a dream visit or by another type of afterlife contact.

The good news is, if you have received a comforting afterlife sign or dream visit from a loved one, whose soul you have been worried about for whatever reason, **you can stop worrying.** Your loved one was only able to visit you because they are residing peacefully in Heaven. That is because only souls in Heaven are given supernatural powers and God's permission to visit us. These afterlife visits are a gift from God's heart to comfort yours.

Anger at God

It is not unusual to blame God for letting sufferings happen and for taking your loved one away from you. It can be a time of crisis in your faith and wondering how a loving God could be so mean. But as explained so eloquently in the book *Glimpses of Heaven From the Angels Who Live There*, by Sunni Welles and her angels, we have all made individual spiritual contracts with God before we came down to earth. We volunteered for our lessons, challenges and missions, and the way we would return Home to God. We don't remember these spiritual agreements until we return back Home, though.

God, the Giver and Taker of life, honors His part of your spiritual contract with Him, by helping you to fulfill it if you ask Him to. God knows when it is the perfect time to bring you back Home and the ripple effect for good it is going to have. Once Home, our memories of our spiritual contracts are fully restored and we are actually very grateful to God for allowing us the experiences we chose for our earthly lives, in order to help us and others grow spiritually stronger and closer to Him.

When you are feeling angry concerning the circumstances surrounding your loved one's death and for taking your loved one away from you, ask God for His help anyway. By asking for God's help, He will shower you with His spiritual support to assist you in your acceptance, healing, comfort, and recovery. Remember, you are not privy to your loved one's soul agreement with God. Try to let go of your anger at God, even though you don't understand the reasons why right now. Eventually all will be revealed to you back in Heaven. In the meantime, God is your greatest Source of healing, so don't deny yourself this healing even if you are angry at God. Ask God to help you to let go of your anger and to heal your heart.

God's understands your anger and pain. Lean on God even

though you may be very angry with Him right now. Cry on your Heavenly Daddy or your Heavenly Brother's shoulder and confide your feelings to Him. He wants you to. He wants to mend your broken heart. Ask Him to.

God hears all our prayers and knows our pain. He looks at the eternal perspective of our souls when He responds to our prayers. It can be so frustrating when God's answer is no, but that is because God has something better in mind for us. God sees the future and knows if what we are asking for will hinder or advance our souls' progress. God sees the bigger picture at all times. He always has the best interest of our eternal souls in mind. Try to trust in God's divine providence and love on your behalf. You are very special to God.

In my bereavement support work, I have noticed there is a striking difference between those who lean on God and those who don't in times of tragedies. Those who turn to God seem to get through their painful heartbreak to a place of peace much more quickly.

Even though I was not angry at God when I lost a 4-month-old pregnancy, and then years later when my father and then my mother passed, I could hardly breathe without feeling a pain in my chest because of my grief. So after my mother passed, I knew that my mother and God wanted me to be happy again, and I desperately wanted to be happy again. So I found myself saying this little prayer when the pain would wash over me, "Dear Jesus, please replace my heart's sorrow with Your joy." Every time I would say that prayer, my heart felt a little better and better and better. Finally, the pain completely left me. It was rather miraculous. I cannot stress enough how directly asking for God to heal you can really help.

* * *

AFTER-DEATH COMMUNICATIONS

* * *

CHAPTER 30

Grief Healing Advice

> The LORD is my shepherd, I shall not be in want. He makes me lie down in green pastures, he leads me beside quiet waters, he restores my soul. He guides me in paths of righteousness for his name's sake. Even though I walk through the valley of the shadow of death, I will fear no evil, for you are with me; your rod and your staff, they comfort me. You prepare a table before me in the presence of my enemies. You anoint my head with oil; my cup overflows. Surely goodness and love will follow me all the days of my life, and I will dwell in the house of the LORD forever (Psalm 23).

Is My Loved One Okay?

When we make the transition from our physical to our spiritual bodies, we are much more alive than when we were here on earth in our limited physical ones. Like a beautiful pearl releasing from its heavy shell, our spirit-souls are released and free and can do things we could only dream of before—like flying. Many who have had near-death experiences who were sent back to earth like Betty Eadie, who describes her wondrous travels through the tunnel to the Light, her tour of Heaven and meeting God in her enlightening book *Embraced by the Light*, were very reluctant to leave God and Heaven to return to earth to finish out their missions. They wanted to stay with God. They didn't want to leave the all-encompassing love and peace they felt and remembered while temporarily being back Home with their Creator. Once you have received a comforting afterlife sign from your loved one, you can stop worrying about them. Only spirits who are in Heaven have supernatural powers and permission from God to contact you.

Who Met My Loved One?

When we cross over to God, we get to reunite with those spirits who will bring us the most comfort to meet and greet us, including our pets.

Talk to Them

Remember, anytime you talk to or even think about your loved one, they instantly hear you loud and clear! So please continue to talk to them or write them letters—for they love the communication from you!

They Still See And Hear You

Your loved ones know everything about your daily life and will continue to for all time. They never miss a birth, christening, birthday, wedding, anniversary, first day of school, graduation or any other important event in your life. They celebrate with us! This is because God values families, love, and the bonds of love that tie us all together as one.

If you could see with spiritual eyes, you would see how very crowded your room is, just filled with your loved ones' spiritual presence and God's angels. Try to visualize this scene, for it is true. You are never alone. Try to think about your loved one as an angel on your shoulder watching over you. From what I have learned in my own spiritual work, it may very well be that they actually are your own personal angel.

Our Children

Spirits in Heaven choose who their own parents will be, as well as their diseases and disabilities. (See Chapter 29 on Soul Agreements.) Children who leave earth at an early age have made these agreements ahead of time while in Heaven with God and their soul group families. They do this for the highest spiritual growth of their soul group members while here on earth, in order to bring them closer to God. Many times these children are Angels Unaware. The spiritual topics Angels Unaware, soul group families, and blueprints of our lives, among many others, are beautifully explained in greater detail in the fascinating and spiritually revealing book *Glimpses of Heaven From the Angels Who Live There*, by Sunni Welles, a Christian spiritual medium (www.sunniwelles.com).

Children in Heaven are taken care of by those they would most hope to be with, e.g. family members, angels, and other soul group members they are connected to. Our children may choose to continue to stay children while growing up in Heaven, and there is a realm for that purpose, too, if that is their choice. Their families are always near in a moment's thought though, so there is no separation.

Where Do Pets Go?

There is a heavenly realm where animals predominately reside. They can also choose to be with the spirits who they already know and love. Those spirits who want to be with their pets can choose to be with them, too, when they return back Home.

God often sends the spirits of our pets to visit us here on earth, and also to greet us when we pass over. I personally have had pet dogs, a chicken, and a cockatiel visit me after they died. These visits to me were in visions and in dreams.

Goodbye, I Love You & Forgiveness

If you want an ongoing spiritual relationship with a loved one, then say goodbye to the physical them, but hello to the new spiritual relationship you desire to have with them now. This can also be done by writing a letter to your loved one.

Our loved ones live on and are still with us in their beautiful spiritual bodies, all the while loving and trying to comfort us. We never "die" in the real sense. The spirit's soul, the true essence of who we are, lives on even, though invisible to our human eyes.

However, if you are feeling regret because you did not have an opportunity to say goodbye, I love you, thank you, I forgive you, or to apologize to them for wrongs you are sorry for, or any other emotions and feelings, it is never too late to do this, for they hear you now too!

Writing a letter to them can immensely help purge the pent-up emotions you are feeling. It helps to finally get those unspoken words out of your system. Have a smiling photo of them when you write your letter. Reading it out loud to them will bring them to you. If you need to forgive them for hurts done to you—and if you do forgive them—it will help you let go of that inner turmoil and move on in peace (forgiving does not mean you are condoning their actions). Once they are back Home, they truly desire your forgiveness for they now see how their actions impacted and hurt you. They see this in a new and understanding Light, with spiritual eyes now, and they are very sorry for those hurts they caused you and others.

Happily Remembering Them

Many times our loved ones will wait until we leave the room to make their transition. They do this out of consideration for you, because they may not have wanted your last memory of them to be such an agonizing one, which may cause you more pain by replaying it over and over in your mind. They hope that you can look beyond any suffering you saw in the past, and instead visualize them as they are now—out of pain, young again, flying by their thoughts, and happy to be back Home with God.

It is very helpful to keep a photo nearby of when your loved one was whole, healthy and joyful. The photo will be an important reminder to keep you focused on the marvelous way they exist now. If you find yourself looking back and hurting over any suffering they had experienced, the photo will be a valuable asset to return your thoughts to the truth of how they are living now. They are no longer locked in that time zone of pain that you remember. They are living a beautiful and joyful life with God now. Because of this, they don't want you to be haunted by dwelling on a time of suffering that no longer exists for them. They want you to be happy for them instead.

Watching home movies of them can be comforting too. Many times they will come and sit with you while you do!

Remember you can still say goodbye, I love you, and talk to them at any time, for they still hear you!

The Hug Pillow and Quilt

You can make a "hug pillow" to use on those days when you need a hug. Simply take a photo of them and have it transferred onto a piece of cloth and then sew it onto a pillow. You can hug that pillow when you are in need, and you can sleep with it, too. Also, you can make a quilt out of their clothes, or pieces of their clothing. Either sew their clothing all together or simply sew the clothes on top of a quilt. This is another snugly way to feel close to them.

Journal Your ADCs

Keep a journal to jot down these cherished after-death communications, for you are making new memories now. If you keep a journal of our new spiritual experiences with our loved ones, you will continue to build pleasant memories to reflect upon to warm your heart on those lonely days and nights.

Laughter

The healing benefits of laughter are priceless. Try to be around people who make you laugh. Rent comedies to help you laugh. Look for any wholesome outlet that will make you laugh and will replace some of your sorrow. Eventually, over time, the sorrow will start to lessen and more happiness and laughter will begin to fill your heart and your life. Laughing does not mean that you have forgotten your loved one. Actually it gives them even more joy to see you happy! Never feel guilty about feeling happy. Our world needs more joy! When you are up to it, try to spread a little joy. It will have the rebound effect of giving your heart more joy in the process.

Feeling Guilty About Reinvesting in Life

Your loved one wants you to reinvest in life and to live a happy and fulfilling one, especially because they are happy and whole being back Home with God. Enjoying and reinvesting in life, until you reunite spirit-to-spirit, does not mean that you have forgotten them! They KNOW this. Never feel guilty about rejoining the human race and living with joy in your heart again. Your loved one desires this for you! They want you to successfully complete your own spiritual lessons on earth too.

They are not jealous or possessive in their spirit bodies and only want the very best for you, as does God. This may even include remarrying. Your loved one may even help to arrange a meeting of a new companion just for that purpose! Remarrying may even be part of your spiritual contract. When you are happy, it makes your loved one even more happy!

Service to Others

Many people who have experienced a devastating loss in their lives over time have been able to turn it around for good by helping others who are newly undergoing the same heartbreak. Who better to understand than one who has already survived the loss of a loved one? When you are healed sufficiently to be able to offer support to others, you are performing in an angelic way that will make God, your angels, and your loved ones very proud of you. Service to others will give you a sense of purpose in your life as well as a sense of meaning concerning your loved one's transition. Your loved ones' returning Home before you, can bring out the best in you and the reason why you are here. Service is a blessing to you and a balm to your heart, as well as to those whose lives you touch. I highly recommend reading *Mother Teresa: In My Own Words*, by González-Balado.

Wanting More Afterlife Signs

At times, God sends our loved ones on important missions. When they are on an important mission, they still know what is happening in your life; however, they may be concentrating very hard on their particular mission, so they may desire to wait till after their mission is completed to contact you again.

Spirits have jobs in Heaven and also spend time learning so that they will be able to advance to even higher realms and closeness to God. There may be a temporary lull in afterlife contacts because of their work and their learning process. But they still are watching over you.

Another reason why you may not receive afterlife contacts as often as you desire them, may be because your loved one does not want to be a distraction from your reinvesting in life. It does not mean that they are not with you or have forgotten about you at all. Our loved ones never forget about us and are always aware of our lives and are forever connected to us. They are part of our soul group connection. They eagerly look forward to the time we will reunite.

However, if you desire to receive an afterlife sign or dream visit, please read Chapter 3 for tips, but a short version is this:

1. Pray to God to allow your loved one to visit you in a comforting way.
2. State something specific to your loved one that you would recognize as a sign from them, e.g. a type of bird.

Spiritual Mediums

Many people have asked me about using a medium. I have seen many, many people find enormous relief and joy and start on the road to healing after using a reputable spiritual medium. This was especially so if they did not feel they were receiving or noticing any afterlife signs. As I explained in Chapter 2 (Spiritual Communication in the Bible), I whole-heartedly believe that some people are gifted by the Holy Spirit to communicate with spirits and angels. It is important though that the spiritual medium know how to discern spirits and to ask for the God-Christ's protection.

The medium that I can highly recommend, who is my very dear and trusted friend, my radio co-host, and author of *Glimpses of Heaven From the Angels Who Live There,* is Sunni Welles. Sunni is a Christian Spiritual Medium who does phone sessions for people of all faiths, such as Christians, Catholics, priests, rabbis, ministers, Muslims, Metaphysical, and New Age Thinkers. She has been gifted to be able to connect to the "specific" spirit her clients request. I always feel so relieved when someone uses Sunni because she is of the highest integrity and extremely gifted. I have had many sessions with her to speak with my parents, my in-laws, and my guardian angel. You can read about Sunni Welles and make a phone appointment with her directly through her website www.sunniwelles.com.

Grieving

Your loved ones are especially with you when you are grieving because you need their comfort. If your loved one visits you in a comforting way, please don't fear that they have not moved on to the Light, for our loved ones in spirit have supernatural powers now that they are back in Heaven. Because of this, they can be with God and with you too (as the apparitions from recognized saints have shown us). These after-death communications are demonstrations of God's love for you to help sustain you until you spiritually reunite with your loved one and God again.

There are many stages of grief and it is normal to go back and forth through different stages and even skip some altogether. The stages and the timing of them are not set in stone. These emotions and pain need to be dealt with, felt, and gone through in order to release your feelings to eventually safely lessen your pain, feel at peace, and heal your heart, so that you will be able to live life to the fullest again as much as possible.

However, even though this is a painful time, the pain does lessen over time. It will get better. You can get help through sharing your feelings with good friends, family members, professionals, therapists, grief support groups, clergy and writing your loved ones letters.

But no matter who you turn to in your time of grief, please remember that your loving Creator is always there waiting to help and comfort you, if you just ask Him to. We can be supported, sustained, and even strengthened through our most profound grief by leaning on and calling upon God for His help—by sharing our heartache with Him. We are never alone. Pray for His soothing peace and comfort to fill your heart. Pray for acceptance in all of this. Pray for joy to one day fill your heart again, until you meet again.

As I mentioned, the very powerful prayer I prayed after my mother died was, "Dear Jesus, please replace my heart's sorrow with Your joy." This prayer was a balm to my heart and soul, and eventually joy did fill my heart much quicker than I expected.

Pray for comforting signs from your loved one. God wants to give all of these gifts to you because He loves you deeply. You are His dear children—His cherished "kids."

Earth is a Temporary Residence

Our earth time is just a very short time span, compared to all eternity. Earth was never intended to be a permanent dwelling for us, more like a summer residence. Earth is where we briefly come to learn lessons, to help others, and to grow spiritually closer to God. Once we complete these learning lessons successfully on earth and return Home, we receive our rewards from God. We can then ascend to a higher realm in Heaven in our permanent, one true Home, back with God and our loved ones again.

Even though you are greatly missing your loved ones, your loved ones in Heaven know that you will be together again. In the meantime, they are like angels on your shoulders trying to guide and help you in life. You are never alone. God, your angel team, and your loved ones are with you always. Once you return Home when your work on earth is done, you will be hugging spirit-to-spirit again. They will greet you as you enter into Heaven, your permanent Home.

Dying is not a tragedy for the one whose spirit-soul releases from their physical body. It is a time of joy, awe and celebration for them. Our loved ones have courageously paved the way for us and are waiting to joyfully greet us. We have a lot to look forward to! The Best Is Yet To Come!

May God bless you and may He wrap His loving arms around each and every one of you. May He replace your heart's sorrow with His joy, and may He comfort all of you with His healing gift of love: after-death communications.

In Christ's Love,

CHRISTINE DUMINIAK
Certified Grief Recovery Specialist
Founder - Prayer Wave For After-Death Communication
Facebook Group: After Death Communications And Prayer Wave
www.christineduminiak.com

* * *

Resources

Recommended Medium:

Sunni Welles, International Christian Spiritual Medium, author and radio cohost. www.sunniwelles.com

Recommended Grief Support Websites:

After Death Communications and Prayer Wave Facebook Group
https://www.facebook.com/groups/Afterdeathcommunicationsprayerwave/

The Compassionate Friends - https://www.compassionatefriends.org/

Open to Hope - http://www.opentohope.com/

Chapel of the Four Chaplains (Emergency Chaplains)
http://www.fourchaplains.org/emergency-chaplains-corps/

Veterans & Family Resources:

Vet to Veterans Assistance - Phone: 1-888-777-4443
https://nvf.org/veteran-resources
https://nvf.org/veterans-request-assistance

Veterans Crisis Line – Phone: 1-800-273-8255 (Press 1) Text to 838255
https://www.veteranscrisisline.net/GetHelp/ResourceLocator.aspx

Warrior Songs - https://www.warriorsongs.org/

TAPS (Tragic Assistance Programs for Survivors Of Armed Forces)
1-800-959-8277
http://www.taps.org/

Recommended Reading:

Heaven Talks To Children: Afterlife Contacts, Spiritual Gifts and Loving Messages – 2nd edition by Christine Duminiak, Ferndale, WA: AlyBlue Media, 2016

Grammy Visits From Heaven by Christine Duminiak, Ferndale, WA: AlyBlue Media, 2015

Grandpa Visits From Heaven by Christine Duminiak, Ferndale, WA: AlyBlue Media, 2017

After-Death Communications: God's Gift of Love by Christine Duminiak, Ferndale, WA: AlyBlue Media, 2017

Grief Diaries: Hello From Heaven by Lynda Cheldelin Fell, Christine Duminiak, Mary Lee Robinson, Ferndale, WA: AlyBlue Media, 2016

Glimpses of Heaven from the Angels Who Live There by Sunni Welles, Philadelphia, PA: Xlibris, 2003

Embraced by the Light by Betty Eadie, Placerville, CA: Gold Leaf Press, 1992

The Walking Wounded by Donna Bowman, Scotts Valley, CA: CreateSpace, 2008

Saved by the Light by Dannion Brinkley and Paul Perry, New York: Harper Paperbacks, 1994

Hear His Voice by Nancy Clark, Frederick, MD: Publish America, 2005

Mysteries Marvels Miracles: In the Lives of Saints by Joan Cruz, Rockford, IL: Tan Books, 1997

One Last Time by John Edward, New York: Berkley, 1998

Religion for Dummies by Rabbi Marc Gellman and Msgr. Thomas Hartman, New York: Wiley, 2003

Hello From Heaven by Bill Guggenheim and Judith Guggenheim, New York: Bantam, 1996

Dialogue with the Dead Is Feasible Vatican Spokesman Says, by John Hooper, London Observer Service. January 1997

Seven Types of Ghosts: A Catholic, Biblical Perspective by Bro. John-Paul Ignatius, Order of the Legion of St. Michael, 2001

When Children Grieve by John James, Russell Friedman, and Leslie Matthews, New York: HarperCollins, 2001

Angels (and Demons): What Do We Really Know About Them? by Peter Kreeft, Ft. Collins, CO: Ignatius Press, 1995

On Life After Death by Elisabeth Kübler-Ross, Berkeley, CA: Celestial Arts, 1991

After Death Communications: Final Farewells by Dr. Louis LaGrand, St. Paul, MN: Llewellyn, 1997

Love Lives On by Dr. Louis LaGrand, New York: Berkley, 2006

Visitations from the Afterlife by Lee Lawson, New York: HarperCollins, 2000

Life After Life by Raymond Moody, New York: Bantam, 1979

Closer to the Light by Morse and Perry, New York: Villard Books, 1990

Transformed by The Light by Melvin Morse and Paul Perry, New York: Villard Books, 1992

Children and Grief by Joey O'Connor, Grand Rapids, MI: Fleming H. Revell, 2004

90 Minutes in Heaven by Don Piper with Cecil Murphey, Grand Rapids, MI: Fleming H. Revell, 2004

Faith in the Departed by Lisa Schneider, May 2005, www.beliefnet.com (accessed December 23, 2009)

Angels Over Their Shoulders by Brad Steiger and Sherry Steiger, New York, NY: Ballantine Books, 1995

My Descent into Death: A Second Chance at Life by Rev. Howard Storm, New York, NY: Doubleday, 2005

Apparitions of Modern Saints by Patricia Treece, Ann Arbor, MI: Servant, 2001

Before I Got Here by Blair Underwood, New York: Atria Books, 2005

Talking to Heaven by James Van Praagh, New York: Dutton, 1997

Visits From Heaven by Josie Varga, Virginia Beach: 4th Dimension Press, 2009.

Acknowledgements

To my dear friend, Jenny Flores—Thank you, dearest Jenny, for always being there to support me when I needed a friend. You gave Prayer Wave For After-Death Communication a Website and a Message Board on the Internet when we needed a home to meet to continue God's healing work. You are wonderful! May God bless you in everything you do.

To my dear Prayer Wave Family—Thank you for being there to give encouragement, hope, love, and prayers to help heal the other grievers who come to Prayer Wave. Because of all of you, Prayer Wave For After-Death Communication has become a haven for healing and uplifting. Thank you for so generously sharing your stories in this book to spread the word that ADCs are a gift from God to help us heal.

To Sunni Welles—My dearest soul sister and mentor, your endless support, help, guidance and love, throughout my mission, have been invaluable to me. You have been an inspiration and a role model to me in your genuine unwavering love, trust, and dedication to the Lord, no matter what the circumstances. Sunni, you are a shining Light in this world and in my life. I deeply cherish our friendship and thank God for you!

To Fred Wright—Thank you my special British friend and extremely gifted healer for taking me under your professional wing to help increase my knowledge of healing. You have been an enormous blessing to me.

To my parents—Ann and Stan Rugel—Thank you, Mom and Dad, for always believing in and encouraging me. Your belief and trust in me and in my spiritual experiences have been a rock in my life. I treasure you both and thank God for blessing me with such wonderful, loving parents. You are the best! A special thanks to you, Daddy-O, and Mom for all the fabulous ADCs of love and fun you have been giving me.

To my in-laws—John and Stella Duminiak—Thank you for opening up the door to my mission on earth by your gentle, but spectacular, spiritual appearance in my bedroom in 1998. Thanks for the many laughs as well as the endless support you have given on earth and from above.

To my Angel Team—Thank you, my dear Angel Team. Your help and tender ways in which you continually guide and protect me, touches my heart so. I thank God for assigning such wonderful and loving angels to me. What would I do without you?

To Jax—Thank you for coming to my rescue and so generously taking on the artistic task of painting my vision for the cover of this book. You have beautifully captured and honored the Holy Spirit's majestic essence. I know God will abundantly bless you in your "Visions of Heaven" artistic work that you are doing for Him, which gives us a peek into the beauty of Heaven.

To Judith Guggenheim—Thank you for being a port in the storm for me, Judith, when I didn't know where to turn. Bill's and your pioneering work on ADCs, enabled me to finally put a meaningful label on my own spiritual experiences. May God bless you for enlightening and comforting so many.

To Lynda Cheledin Fell, my amazing publisher, and a very, very special woman. You are *the* most loving, giving and compassionate person. I feel so blessed to have you in my life and to call you my dear friend. Thank you from the bottom of my heart for everything that you have done for me and for so many others through your huge, caring heart and through AlyBlue Media. I love you, Lynda! God bless you.

To my precious hubby, Bob, and our precious children, Jamie and Matt. I could not have asked for a more wonderful, loving family anywhere! I love you guys with all of my heart. You are the best!

Thank You, God, for my precious family!

CHRISTINE DUMINIAK

About Christine Duminiak

CHRISTINE DUMINIAK is a Certified Grief Recovery Specialist, a radio co-host, an International Spiritual Bereavement Recovery Facilitator and an expert on afterlife signs and contacts. She is the founder and spiritual adviser of the Facebook group: After Death Communication and Prayer Wave, a nondenominational online grief support and prayer group.

Duminiak is a member of the National Alliance for Grieving Children and has been in the field of spiritual bereavement support since 1998. She is the author of *After-Death Communications: God's Gift of Love; Grammy Visits From Heaven; Grandpa Visits From Heaven; Heaven Talks To Children,* and the co-author of *Grief Diaries: Hello From Heaven.* She is the creator and voice of the guided meditation CD titled *Meditation of God's Love and Healing: For Those Who Grieve.*

Duminiak is a frequent guest speaker in James Van Praagh's chat room. Her book and grief support and prayer group are recommended by James Van Praagh for grief support and understanding the afterlife.

Duminiak frequently speaks at The Learning Annex in New York City, to The Compassionate Friends, to Mothers Against Drunk Driving (MADD), to Rotary Clubs, a Keynote Speaker at National Conventions, to senior citizen groups, spirituality groups, to bereavement groups, children's groups, veterans, Gold Star Families, colleges, and to the general public.

A Certified Reflexologist and a Certified Energy Healing Practitioner, Duminiak has volunteered her time and skills to hospice and cancer patients, for women in crisis pregnancies shelters, and for women transitioning from substance abuse shelters.

MEDIA:

Duminiak has been an expert guest on Fox and Friends; the Fox News Strategy Room; Fox's Good Day Philadelphia; NBC 12 TV the Arizona Midday show in Phoenix; on Philadelphia's NBC 10 TV talk show 10!; on the news on NBC 10 TV; on the news on CBS 3 TV in Philadelphia; on Telecare TV, Diocese of Rockville Centre, New York on The God Squad with Msgr. Tom Hartman and Rabbi Marc Gellman; on Open To Hope TV, on talk radio shows, including the nationally syndicated Coast to Coast AM; and in The Philadelphia Inquirer, The Bucks County Courier Times, The Arizona Republic, The East Valley Tribune (Scottsdale), and The Reporter in the Villages (Florida).

Visit her website at www.christineduminiak.com. and email her at chrisduminiak@aol.com

ALYBLUE MEDIA TITLES

PUBLISHED
Grammy Visits From Heaven
Grandpa Visits From Heaven
Heaven Talks to Children
God's Gift of Love: After Death Communication
Faith, Grief & Pass the Chocolate Pudding
Real Life Diaries: Living with Mental Illness
Real Life Diaries: Living with Endometriosis
Real Life Diaries: Living with Rheumatic Disease
Real Life Diaries: Living with a Brain Injury
Real Life Diaries: Through the Eyes of DID
Real Life Diaries: Through the Eyes of an Eating Disorder
Grief Diaries: Surviving Loss of a Spouse
Grief Diaries: Surviving Loss of a Child
Grief Diaries: Surviving Loss of a Sibling
Grief Diaries: Surviving Loss of a Parent
Grief Diaries: Surviving Loss of an Infant
Grief Diaries: Surviving Loss of a Loved One
Grief Diaries: Surviving Loss by Suicide
Grief Diaries: Surviving Loss of Health
Grief Diaries: How to Help the Newly Bereaved
Grief Diaries: Loss by Impaired Driving
Grief Diaries: Loss by Homicide
Grief Diaries: Loss of a Pregnancy
Grief Diaries: Hello from Heaven
Grief Diaries: Grieving for the Living
Grief Diaries: Shattered
Grief Diaries: Project Cold Case
Grief Diaries: Poetry & Prose and More
Grief Diaries: Through the Eyes of Men
Grief Diaries: Will We Survive?
Grief Diaries: Hit by Impaired Driver
Color My Soul Whole
Grief Reiki

To share your story in a Grief Diaries book,
visit www.griefdiaries.com

PUBLISHED BY ALYBLUE MEDIA
Inside every human is a story worth sharing.
www.AlyBlueMedia.com

www.ingramcontent.com/pod-product-compliance
Lightning Source LLC
Chambersburg PA
CBHW071558080526
44588CB00010B/948